the collected poe[ms of]
Abdullah Quilliam

An official seal in silver designed by the Imperial Ottoman Arsenal that arrived in Liverpool in August 1895. Afzal Kaduji of Kad Design, Manchester, has recreated the seal from a stamp made by the original. The stamp was found in the Ottoman archives, preserved in correspondence sent by Quilliam in 1896 about the Sudan crisis, asking for a confirmation of his fatwa from the Ottoman Şeyhülislâm Mehmed Cemaleddin. The stamp reads "(Al-)Shaykh Abdullah Quilliam".

(*TC*, 14/08/1895, p.105; BOA Y.PRK.MS,6/41.)

the collected poems of
Abdullah Quilliam

Edited by
Ron Geaves and Yahya Birt

BEACON BOOKS

First published in the UK by Beacon Books and Media Ltd
Earl Business Centre, Dowry Street, Oldham OL8 2PF UK.

First edition published in 2021

www.beaconbooks.net

ISBN   978-1-912356-89-8 Paperback
ISBN   978-1-912356-90-4 Hardback
ISBN   978-1-912356-91-1 Ebook

Cataloging-in-Publication record for this book is available from the British Library

Cover concept by Yahya Birt and design by Raees M. Khan

CONTENTS

ABDULLAH QUILLIAM (1856–1923) is among the most well-known of early British converts to Islam. Following his conversion in 1887, he established Britain's first Islamic centre in his home city. The Liverpool Muslim Institute consisted of a mosque, two Muslim schools, a printing press, an orphanage and a museum, and provided various educational activities for locals. In addition to his professional activities as a Liverpool lawyer and journalist, he was a polymath who lectured on geology, theology, comparative religion and the history of the ancient world. His weekly newspaper *The Crescent*, in which he published much of the poetry in the present collection, ran from 1893 to 1908 and circulated to over eighty nations.

RON GEAVES is a retired professor of religion better known for his academic writing in the study of religion. He remains a visiting professor in the Centre for the Study of Islam in the UK based in the School of History, Archaeology and Religion at the University of Cardiff. In 2010 he published *Islam in Victorian Britain: The Life and Times of Abdullah Quilliam* (Kube Press) and in 2017 *Victorian Muslim: Abdullah Quilliam and Islam in the West* (Hurst). In 2017 he published *Rumi Weeds* (Beacon Books), his first collected volume of poetry.

YAHYA BIRT is a community historian who has taught at the University of Leeds. He has an M.Phil. in Social and Cultural Anthropology from the University of Oxford. He has published over a dozen peer-reviewed articles on Islam in Britain and co-edited *British Secularism and Religion: Islam, Society and State* (Markfield: Kube, 2016) and *Islam in Victorian Liverpool: An Ottoman Account of Britain's First Mosque Community* (Swansea: Claritas Books, 2021). He lives in West Yorkshire with his family and two cats. He likes walking and being grumpy about the state of the world. He can be reached on Twitter @ybirt.

ABBREVIATIONS

AR   *The Allahabad Review* (Allahabad, 1890–5)

CE   Common Era (the Gregorian calendar)

DJA   *The Dunfermline Journal and Advertiser for the West of Fife* (Dunfermline, 1800–1932)

EI2   Edited by P. J. Bearman et al., *Encyclopædia of Islam*, 2nd Edition., 12 vols. with indexes, etc., Leiden: E. J. Brill, 1960–2005; online edition: 2012.

H   Anno Hegirae ("in the year of the Hijra"); the Islamic calendar

Hymns *A Collection of Hymns Suitable for use at the Meetings of the English Speaking Moslem Congregations* (Liverpool: T. Dobb & Co, 1892).

IC   *Islamic Culture* (Hyderabad, 1927–2004)

IR   *Islamic Review* (Woking, 1913–71)

IW   *The Islamic World* (Liverpool, 1893–1908)

OED   *Oxford English Dictionary*, 1st Edition, 1884–1928; 2nd Edition, 1989; 3rd Edition, 2000–.

Sale   George Sale, *The Koran translated into English from the Original Arabic* (London: Frederick Warne & Co., n.d. [1734]).

SAP   H.M. Léon, *Some Arabian Poets* (Regality Press: Dunfermline, 1930). Reprinted from the Dunfermline Journal.

SHA   H.M. Léon, *Sheikh Haroun Abdullah, A Turkish Poet and his Poetry* (Blackburn: Geo. Toulmin & Sons for La Société Internationale de Philologie, Science et Beaux-Arts, 1916).

Slane   Baron MacGuckin de Slane (trans.) *Ibn Khallikan's Biographical Dictionary* (Paris: Oriental Translation Fund of Great Britain and Northern Ireland, 1843–71), 4 vols.

TC   *The Crescent* (Liverpool, 1893–1908)

TP   *The Philomath* (Nottingham–London, 1913–1932)

EDITORS' INTRODUCTION

WHEN WILLIAM HENRY ABDULLAH QUILLIAM (1856–1932) declared his conversion to Islam publicly in 1887, he was not content to merely practise his new faith as did other early British converts of the period. Rather, he set about the task of establishing Islam in Britain, starting with his home city of Liverpool. To this end, he established the Liverpool Muslim Institute and through its various activities converted approximately 250 inhabitants of the city to Islam.[1] Throughout the early 1890s, he developed the first Islamic centre in Britain, which consisted of a mosque, two Muslim schools (male and female), a printing press, an orphanage, a museum, along with various educational activities for local Liverpool youth to better themselves. His weekly newspaper *The Crescent* was published from 1893 to 1908 and circulated to over eighty nations. His efforts to promote Islam were recognised by the Caliph, Sultan Abdul-Hamid II, and by Abdur-Rahman, the Amir of Afghanistan, and both bestowed various titles, honours and gifts upon him and his family and they were named as patrons of the Liverpool Muslim Institute.

Born in 1856 to a respectable upper-middle class family, whose ancestry included a naval officer who had commanded the *HMS Victory* at the Battle of Trafalgar and another who owned one of Liverpool's best-known clock-manufacturing companies, William Henry had been a precocious child. Attending the well-known Liverpool Institute where he won national prizes for his interest in geology, he became famous for his involvement alongside his parents and grandparents at Temperance Society meetings throughout the North-West. As a young teenager he was already known to the Liverpool media as the 'Temperance child' after a number of passionate speeches condemning alcohol. He was to be an outspoken critic and supporter of temperance throughout his life and it may have played a part in his conversion to Islam and his visit to Morocco in 1883. Abdullah Quilliam was renowned in Liverpool for his philanthropic work. He was the President of the significant dockside Carters Union,[2] a campaigner for the abolition of capital punishment, an active supporter of Negro rights in the USA, a one-time editor of the satirical magazine *The Porcupine* and *The Good Templar*, a Temperance movement publication. Famously, he was a skilled lawyer who advocated for Liverpool's poor, especially the women of the rapidly expanding dockside communities, defended a number of notorious murderers and prided himself that he had saved many from the gallows. The *Liverpool Weekly Courier* described him as the "unofficial Attorney-General of Liverpool".[3] His trade union activities went beyond leadership of the Carters Union, and he represented the journeyman bakers, upholsterers, brickmakers, coppersmiths and the Lancashire Sea Fisheries at various times in his legal career.

Abdullah Quilliam was a man of immense physical and mental energy. In addition to his professional activities, he was also a polymath who lectured on geology, theology, comparative religion and the history of the ancient world. On his conversion to Islam, he would apply the same intellectual, creative and activist energies to the promotion of his new faith.

As a well-known Liverpool lawyer and journalist, his expertise in both fields made him an accomplished advocate for his new faith. He had established a printing press in 1893 with donations from Muslim well-wishers in British India and Malaya, which allowed him to publish his weekly newspaper, *The Crescent,* and a monthly journal, *The Islamic World.*[4] Both were distributed to Muslim nations but, above all else, they were key to establishing the tone for Quilliam's efforts to reposition the understanding of Islam and its place in the religious history of the world to the British public. Quilliam's community was led by converts and with his genius they sought to establish Islam according to the best norms of the society around them. Quilliam did not consider Islam to be a religion of foreigners or associated with ethnicity. Above all else, it was an ancient path that led to being in tune with an omniscient Creator, and as such could be adapted to any time or civilisation. In his time, he sought ways to establish Islam that chimed with what he saw as the best values of Victorian Britain, and so he promoted the best values of Victorian society as synonymous with Islam.

Quilliam initially propagated Islam from rented premises in Liverpool's Mount Vernon Street but enjoyed little success. His original approach had been to compare the shortcomings of Christianity with the strengths of Islam, but this had led to him being maligned or ridiculed, especially by audiences of irate Christians who would attend his lectures with the intention to disrupt them.[5] Quilliam never gave up on this comparative approach and *The Crescent* reveals that he continued his direct attack on Christianity, especially upon the prevailing attitudes that existed in Victorian society towards Islam. However, alongside this approach, he added a more indirect method of attracting audiences to hear him, one that avoided direct persuasion.

It was mainly at his public services and lectures delivered on Sunday evenings at the new premises in Brougham Terrace that Quilliam attracted his converts to Islam. He did not preach but spoke on a number of topics that displayed his remarkable breadth of knowledge. Before the lectures, the Muslim converts would gather and sing the well-known hymns of Nonconformist and Anglican Christianity rewritten by Quilliam to ensure that they were in accord with Islamic monotheism. By 1908, Quilliam was known nationally and throughout the Muslim world. He had also converted around two hundred and fifty individuals to Islam in his home city and possibly several hundred further afield. Many of the converts were drawn from the professional and upper-middle classes of the city but many were tradesmen and also from amongst the city's numerous clerks.

Most of Quilliam's Sunday lectures are reproduced in *The Crescent* along with political arguments for Britain maintaining closer relationships with the Ottoman Empire and his various topics on Islam and Muslim civilisation. Yet despite all of this activity, he managed to write poetry along with three novels.[6] *The Crescent*'s literary contents show the importance of poetry in the Victorian worldview and Quilliam's own interests. Poetry permitted the Sheikh to draw upon both British and Eastern literary heritages, sometimes combining both in his poetic endeavours. Lectures by the Sheikh reproduced in *The Crescent* include early Arab pre-Islamic poetry and several on well-known British poets. Amongst the contributions by converts there is a lecture on Longfellow by Rosa Warren, "A Sketch of English Literature" by Nuruddin Stephen and "John Dryden: A Great English Poet" attributed to Henri Mustapha Léon.[7]

A Man of Letters

In addition to these lectures, it was rare that an edition of *The Crescent* or Quilliam's journal, *The Islamic World*, appeared without the publication of at least one poem. The poems could be a reprint of a sonnet by Shakespeare or other well-known British or American writers. Most popular were the poems of the Romantics and the Metaphysical Poets. In such cases, their content typically provided inspiration that echoed the universal truths of the wisdom of the world's religions, especially the Abrahamic trinity of Judaism, Christianity, and Islam. Original poems by named and unnamed males and females also appear often, presumably selected by Quilliam as editor. Most interesting for historians of Victorian and early Edwardian Islam in Britain are the poems written by Muslims directly pertaining to Islamic topics, especially those that demonstrated the sentiments felt towards the poet's faith, the founder of Islam or directed in prayer towards Allah. Amongst this latter group are many of the poems of Abdullah Quilliam.

We acknowledge the important collection of convert poets from the period that includes many of Quilliam's Islamic poems, which has been edited by Brent Singleton.[8] Many of these poems have been reproduced on various online forums, but, in this collection, we have gone much further. We have included poems that show Quilliam's love for nature in his ancestral home on the Isle of Man or draw upon its folk literature. There are also poems about historic or topical events, and finally those that reveal the poet's affections, including his romantic interests. In the latter examples, the editors have not indulged the temptation to engage in speculation regarding the object of Quilliam's passion but have included the poems as the author himself elected to publish them. His strong inclinations towards romantic love for women are also revealed in the translations of classical Abbasid poetry that appear in *Islamic Culture* edited by Marmaduke Pickthall in Hyderabad during Quilliam's last decade. Most significantly we have also included the Sheikh's output under the identity of Léon, including those that he identified as translations.[9] Finally, it should be emphasized that while this collection is comprehensive, it is not exhaustive. While there may well have been poems that have escaped our trawl through the primary sources, we also took an editorial decision to exclude couplets and short stanzas or poems, particularly where they are too fragmentary in meaning, i.e. heavily context-dependent, as is sometimes the case with Quilliam's translations in Part 3.

Overall, the poems are typical examples of Victorian sentiment and rarely break free of the conventional confines of rhyme and metre associated with the period except when Quilliam played with translating or imitating classical Islamic poetry from Arabia, Turkey or Persia when he would adapt or adopt Eastern forms such as the *ghazal*. Brought together for the first time, including the later poetry attributed to or published as Henri M. Léon after Quilliam's return from Istanbul, and most significantly the poetry included in *Sheikh Haroun Abdullah, A Turkish Poet and his Poetry* published in 1916,[10] these poems reveal much about the inner life of Britain's most famous Muslim convert and founder of the first mosque community to be established in the UK and they complement other literary output in documenting his life. Abdullah Quilliam may not have been the most accomplished poet among the British convert community that particular accolade must be reserved for John Yahya Parkinson, the Scottish poet and friend of the Sheikh—but Quilliam's poems will always be of historic interest due to the part he played in the history of Islam in Britain and in identifying his personal relationship towards Islam. A good portion of his poetry can be plausibly read as autobiographical: Quilliam often used his poetry to express his deepest feelings about his life, those closest to him, and his faith; as he put it, his "most inmost heart".

Abdullah Quilliam's literary interests identify him as a "man of letters", originally a French term derived from *belletrist* or *homme de lettres*, a label that predated our contemporary usage of intellectual or academic, and referring to a man who is well-versed in literature and related scholarly pursuits. By the nineteenth century, British use of "man of letters" had narrowed down to define a person who earned their living writing intellectually about literature such as an essayist, journalist or critic.[11] To this intellectual endeavour, Quilliam would also add the creative writing of poetry and fiction. Samuel Coleridge coined the term "clerisy" to refer to an intellectual class that functioned to uphold and maintain national culture, a secular equivalent of the Anglican clergy. However, there is an element in which such figures operated as powerful critics of the status quo. The theologian Alister McGrath speaks of an "alienated, theologically literate, anti-establishment lay intelligentsia" that originated in Germany from the 1830s.[12] French intellectuals were also well-established as critics of society after the Revolution of 1789. A similar role developed in Russia in the late nineteenth century. The Romantic movement in Britain saw the poet and critic merge in figures such as Coleridge, Shelley and Byron. By Quilliam's time the intellectual class had become established in public life throughout Europe, including Britain. Often, such self-styled intellectuals would intervene in arts, politics, journalism and education.[13] Jean-Paul Sartre would identify such figures as the "moral conscience of their age; that their moral and ethical responsibilities are to observe the socio-political moment, and to freely speak to their society, in accordance with their consciences".[14] Such figures were usually polymaths and that is certainly true of Quilliam. He could not be identified as secular as in Coleridge's definition, as it would be more appropriate to identify him as "homo religiosis".[15] He would promote Islam as the solution to the ills in society that he identified in his role as a "man of letters", as one among the newly emerging intellectual class. His interest in literature falls within this framework of developing a remarkable strategy to promote Islam and his writings in *The Crescent* and *Islamic World*, can be identified as within this category of writing but there is no doubt that Quilliam's interests lay within or in the realm of the public intellectual of his day.

Quilliam as Henri Marcel Léon

This identification as a man of letters or as an intellectual becomes more overt in Quilliam's later life in London, when he lived under the pseudonym of Henri Marcel Léon. In the absence of his public role as the Sheikh-ul-Islam of the British Isles and the focal point provided by the mosque in Liverpool, Quilliam recreated himself as a public intellectual heading the Société Internationale de Philologie, Sciences et Beaux Arts, publishing the journal *The Philomath*, where he would continue to publish his poems and the poetry of others. Philology is the study of the structure of language or the historical development of a language or languages, and includes textual criticism, literary criticism, history of languages and linguistics. "Beaux-Arts" refers specifically to a school of architecture influential in nineteenth-century France but also refers more generally to the fine arts. Quilliam's new society and livelihood in London show his primary interests in literature, the arts and, of course, the science of geology. Islam offered him the possibility of utilising these interests in both the Arabic and Turkish languages, but also incorporating a body of knowledge from outside the Graeco-Roman traditions. As a scholar of languages, he was particularly interested in the poetic content of the Qur'an and its interpretation but also in the poetic forms of the ancient and contemporary worlds.

Quilliam returned from Istanbul in late 1909 (or possibly earlier), adopting the pseudonym Henri Marcel Léon and an identity as a learned man of letters, which allowed him in his last quarter-century to pursue his passions for philology, comparative religion, geology, literature, history and any other disciplines or topics that attracted his flexible and powerful intellect and roving curiosity. It is tempting to draw the conclusion that William Gottlieb Leitner (1840–99), once his nemesis and rival from Woking, was also a goad and inspiration to Quilliam too as a proximate model of a feted polymath and polyglot.[16] Yet it was an open secret among the small, tight-knit Muslim community that Léon and Quilliam were one and the same person, as it was among his old non-Muslim friends like Hall Caine, but out of respect for the Sheikh they accepted this new identity and did not betray him to wider society.[17] This then was the new public persona that Quilliam had cultivated as Dr Henri M. Léon, the erudite general secretary of a learned society, who took a merely academic interest, *inter alia*, in translating early modern Ottoman poetry.

The period 1908–13 spanned Quilliam's years of crisis. With his departure in 1908, the Liverpool Muslim Institute closed shortly thereafter, leaving the Muslim community to disperse and diminish, without a mosque, an imam or an institute. He was no longer Sheikh-ul-Islam of the British Isles. He lost his professional status when he was struck off as a solicitor in 1909 for fabricating evidence in a divorce case (his friend defended this as an act of gallantry to extricate a woman from a bad marriage). He lost his daughter, Habeeba, at a young age in 1908; her premature death grieved Quilliam immensely as will be discussed below. His hopes of peaceful retirement in Turkey were dashed when his chief patron, caliph-sultan Abdul Hamid II, was overthrown in the Young Turk Revolution. And, although his reasons for doing so are a matter of perennial contention, he lost his public identity as Abdullah Quilliam when he took up the new identity of Dr Léon.

From the little that we know presently about his years back in England from 1909–13, Quilliam as Léon struggled to find steady work and to consolidate his persona in a meaningful way. He worked as an itinerant producer, director and business manager in the provincial theatre from at least April 1910, marketing himself as "the late director-in-chief of amusement for the Sultan of Turkey" and a former actor in Turkey in small towns up and down the country, with an additional role as a public lecturer, using his beloved lantern-slides to entertain audiences.[18] Later published after the First World War, he summed up the struggles of those years in the poem, "Fight On", that he wrote on Christmas Day 1911 and published in Part 1 of this volume:

> Be not dismay'd whate'er betide, Fight on! Fight on!
> Do your best and patiently bide, Fight on! Fight on!
> Thro' days of toil, tho' care assail, Fight on! Fight on!
> The right is sure to yet prevail, Fight on! Fight on!

It was in Nottingham that Léon would develop an "intimate association" and enough support to solidify his new persona as an academician: it was here that his learned society and its journal, *The Philomath*, were successfully launched in 1913, which then enabled him to relocate to London the following year. There he would eventually settle in Bloomsbury and play an active but secondary role with the small Muslim community in London and Woking.[19]

The Poems

This collection is divided into three parts. Part 1 contains individual poems written by Abdullah Quilliam or Henri Marcel Léon and presented in the date order of publication rather than the date of writing as sometimes recorded by the poet. Wherever possible the layout of the poems follows that of the author and preserves the typical, lyrical Victorian style that was used by him.

The earliest poems that begin the collection are taken from *A Collection of Hymns Suitable for use at the Meetings of the English Speaking Moslem Congregations* (Liverpool: T. Dobb & Co) published in 1892. They reveal Quilliam's syncretic approach to the propagation of Islam in late Victorian

Britain and his passion for his newly acquired faith. This 48-page hymnal, of which to date only a sole copy is known to have survived as part of the Pratt Green Collection at the University of Durham Library, is a unique Anglo Islamic-Christian synthesis, that features 52 hymns and captures the nascent practices of the Liverpool Muslim Institute in the early 1890s, and were observed until the community's demise in 1908, alongside a growing commitment to more orthodox Islamic practices of prayer and worship. For our purposes here, only those hymns written by Quilliam are included, which number seven in total, rather than the pre-existing Christian hymns that were slightly or more heavily adapted to make them more "Islamic".

It is not until January 1895 that "Scale Force" appears in *The Crescent*, a major source for the publication of his poetry up to 1908, alongside *The Islamic World* and, at times, the Manx press. This was not Quilliam's first poem to be published in his weekly newspaper but all those from 1894 are presumed lost (with the exception of one long poem preserved elsewhere in *The Allahabad Review*), although copies of his monthly, *The Islamic World*, have survived, and three of his poems were published in it during 1893–4. As with several of the Sheikh's poems, he takes the opportunity to link the theme of the poem to a verse from the Qur'an.[20] The final set of poems in Part 1 were primarily written under his pseudonym Henri Marcel Léon (but also sometimes as Quilliam) and were mostly published in his journal *The Philomath*. These poems were collected principally by Yahya Birt whose research into Quilliam's latter years also unearthed the poems in Parts 2 and 3.

Part 3 consists of the translated poems published under the pseudonym of Haroun Mustapha Léon in *Islamic Culture*, the journal first edited by Marmaduke Pickthall during his years in Hyderabad. They were published in a series of articles on classical Islamic poets and poetry from 1927–31 and constitute the final output of Quilliam before his death in 1932. These translations were published in three places, but the version given here is the one published in *Islamic Culture*. Some of them were serialised in the Dunfermline Journal in 1928, and were later collected together in Henri Marcel Léon, *Some Arabian Poets* (Dunfermline: Regality Press, 1930). The footnotes to these poems largely duplicate Léon's but with a little embellishment from the editors for clarity where needed. With one exception, the poets are real figures, who were nearly all connected with the Abbasid caliphate (750–1258CE) and living or writing at the Baghdad court. It is not always possible to ascertain if the unattributed poetry is Léon's own or whether he is misattributing some of his own poetry to these Abbasid-era court poets, as is certainly the case with the claimed translations of the Turkish poet, Haroun Abdullah, in Part 2.

As already stated, these poems in Part 2 represent the only sole collection by the Sheikh and therefore are also treated separately. A decision was taken to exclude poems published in *The Crescent* with no acknowledged authorship. Usually Quilliam would sign his poems in *The Crescent* to differentiate himself from other poets published in the newspaper, often even signing himself as "Sheikh ul-Islam of the British Isles" and we have chosen to be strict on this matter and publish only those acknowledged by the Sheikh.

Translator or *Maḥlaṣ*?[21]

The exception to this rule is made with the inclusion of the claimed translations of the Turkish poet, Haroun Abdullah. After detailed analysis of the poems, the editors are agreed that their authorship belongs to Quilliam and were written during the Sheikh's sojourns in Istanbul between 1903 and 1908. Quilliam was engaging in *takhallus*,[22] the common use of a pen-name or pseudonym sometimes used by Persian and Urdu poets. *Takhallus* is an Arabic word which means, literally, to become liberated or secure[23] and this would fit easily with Quilliam's balance of public and private life during an uneasy exile. Abdullah Quilliam's departure for Istanbul in 1908 was by no means the end of his published output as a poet, most of which appeared in the journal of the learned society he established in 1913, *The Philomath* of the Société Internationale de Philologie, Sciences et Beaux-Arts and are collected together in Part 1 of this volume. But his most significant poetic output in this period was his only standalone poetry collection, *Sheikh Haroun Abdullah: A Turkish Poet and His Poetry*.

The poems are presented here in their entirety, including those cited in and extracted from its lengthy prose Introduction (pp.13–37 in the original), which comprises of a synopsis on Sufism, a biography of the poet—interspersed with 11 personal or historically significant poems—and a brief literary analysis. Besides the Introduction, the collection is ostensibly a translation of 25 selected poems by a seventeenth-century Mevlevi Sufi poet from Ottoman Turkish into English, divided into four sections of mystic (pp.39–54), historical (pp.55–64), moral (pp.65–84) and miscellaneous poems (pp.85–95). Most of the poems are short, between 10–40 lines; the preferred form is rhyming couplets. The collection is capped by a long glossary explaining the meanings of Turkish, Arabic and Farsi terms used in the poems, which has been used to preserve Quilliam's own translations into English in the footnotes, with any further editorial glosses put in brackets.

Even if considered as translations these poems deserve inclusion in this anthology because they can justly be regarded as part of Quilliam's output as a poet too. In finding the poet Dryden's middle course for poetry in translation between paraphrase and latitude, there is considerable scope to consider the creative freedom and vision of the translator-poet too, who seeks to capture the spirit of the original beyond mere literal paraphrasing.[24] And notwithstanding the considerable number of Turkish words and references in some of these poems, the collection as a whole certainly reflects Quilliam's established range of poetic voices and styles seen elsewhere in this collection.

It would appear that despite this newly solidified persona as Dr Léon, Quilliam clearly chafed at the restraints of his new life and missed his old one. After 1913, it was common practice for him to write pieces in his own journals either as Léon or as Quilliam, and this practice included his poetry too. In addition to these two authorial personas (Léon and Quilliam), we would like to advance the theory that he deployed a *third* pen-name drawing upon the device of *takhallus* used historically, namely, Sheikh Haroun Abdullah. In the opinion of the editors, it is a portmanteau name that refers to his two other identities: Henri Marcel, or *Haroun* Mustapha as he sometimes went by, Léon, combined with *Sheikh* William Henry *Abdullah* Quilliam. Or *Sheikh Haroun Abdullah* for short.

There is a striking amount of internal and external evidence to take the argument seriously that this is Quilliam's own poetry rather than a faithful, scholarly translation by an academician of an early modern Mevlevi poet. From 1914, Quilliam would sometimes use his new public persona as Dr Léon to present his personal devotional poetry as translations "from the Turkish" in his own journal. Some of these are unattributed translations "from the Turkish", while others are attributed to a named individual.[25] On top of this, three poems in this collection have a double attribution, credited firstly to Haroun Mustapha Léon in the *Islamic Review* (Woking) in 1914–5, and secondly as "translations" from Sheikh Haroun Abdullah by Dr Henri Marcel Léon in the 1916 collection.[26] This can be read as claiming authorship of these poems for a Muslim audience while presenting them as scholarly translations for an academic audience.

Dr Léon provides a biographical sketch of Sheikh Haroun Abdullah (ca. 964H/1555–6CE–ca.1047H/1637–8CE) in the Introduction. Born in the former Ottoman capital, Bursa, Haroun memorised the Qur'an at age 10, joins the Mevlevi Order at 14. He becomes fluent in Arabic, Persian and Turkish, memorises 5266 prophetic hadiths, excels in astronomy, medicine and several other sciences, and is known for his piety, rectitude, charity and honour. Sheikh Haroun becomes a prolific composer of short mystical poems, and is known for one long poem, not featured in the collection, "Muhammad bin Qasim"; occasionally he wrote love poetry to his wife, Habeeba Khanoum, who was severely ill for three years before dying at a young age, which affected the Sheikh deeply. Later Sheikh Haroun is banished for several years to Aleppo by the Sultan for a poem, "Al-Miraj", that was read as a scathing critique of the court. Later, his poem, "The Coming of Ertoghrul", is brought to the attention of Sultan Murad Khan IV (r.1631–40), who ends his exile, recalling him to the court. One of his poem's the "Cuckoo Poem" (Kughuk-Kushu) was written in gold, and placed in the Imperial Library at the behest of Sultan Murad. The Sheikh dies at the age of 84 and is buried with full honours at Eyüp Sultan, the tomb of the Prophet's Companion, Abu Ayyub al-Ansari, in Istanbul.

Yet, as detailed and compelling as this story is, no such Mevlevi poet of that name is mentioned in the standard reference work on Mevlevi poets in the Ottoman period that goes up to the eighteenth century, *Tezkire-i Şuarâ-i Mevleviyye (Biographies of Mevlevi Poets)* by Esrar Dede.[27] Nor is there any mention of this Sufi sheikh and poet in Ottoman court records being honoured for his poetry by the sultan or exiled and later rehabilitated, as Léon claims in the Introduction. Rather, the biography of Sheikh Haroun appears to be a composite of biographical elements of notable Mevlevi poets like Nefʿī, who fell out of favour for his satirical writing, Khayālī, whom Sulayman the Magnificent favoured, or Müneccimbaşı, the only Mevlevi poet mentioned in Dede's *Tezkire* to have studied *heyʾet* (astronomy), *nücūm* (astrology), and *ʿilm-i ṭibb u ṭabīʿiyyāt* (medicine and natural sciences).[28] There are also some historical and linguistic discrepancies, but whether these are simple errors, deliberate signals to more learned readers, or a mixture of the two is hard to say for certain.[29] In this regard, the lack of corroborating historical evidence that the sultan admired and honoured named poems like "The Coming of Ertoghrul" or the "Cuckoo Poem" is particularly noteworthy.

There are internal features in the collection that demonstrate a literary style not in keeping with classical Ottoman (divan) poetry; rather, the titles of the poems are more reflective of the Tanzimat period in the latter half of the nineteenth century. Nothing can be said conclusively here as we lack access to the alleged original Turkish poems of Sheikh Haroun Abdullah, other than a few Turkish phrases interspersed throughout the collection. However, there are four general features of classical divan poetry that these poems do not have. Firstly, nowhere does the poet refer to himself by a penname (*maḫlaṣ*), which was the given convention in the classic period: a poet would adopt one right at the beginning of his or her career. It may well be that this very absence is a deliberate clue, pointing towards Sheikh Haroun

Abdullah being the *maḫlaṣ* of Quilliam/Léon. Secondly, odes and poems in the classical period were untitled and only referred to by genre (e.g. *ghazal* or *na't*); only very rarely would a longer piece that became well-known outside of a poet's divan be titled. Yet, in this collection, all the poems are titled. Thirdly, divan poetry developed and then drew upon what became a well-established stock of symbolic themes (*maẓmūn*s). However, commonplace *maẓmūn*s do not appear in this collection. Fourthly, newer *maẓmūn*s appeared in Tanzimat poetry and replaced the older ones. Some of these, like proverbs and animals, do appear in this collection.[30]

Given that in this period Quilliam's dual identity was an open secret to his close friends and allies, his delight in teasing the cognoscenti with allusions, clues, perhaps even deliberate errors, while seeking to delude the rest of his readership by successfully carrying off his persona as Dr Léon, is a persistent feature of his writing.[31] Another example is Léon's deliberate and flagged use of Edward Fitzgerald's thirty-second quatrain, with very minor modifications, from his translated *Rubaiyat* of Omar Khayyam, one of the most famous English language poems in the early twentieth century. Yet while he works directly from Fitzgerald, he presents this as evidence of Khayyam's influence on Sheikh Haroun in the seventeenth century (*SHA*, pp.20, 45)!

The Significance of Sheikh Haroun Abdullah's Poetry

So, if Quilliam is the true author of these poems it affords us new insights into his inner spiritual life as well as his personal travails, if we choose to interpret some of the poems here as veiled biography, hidden behind a *maḫlaṣ*, or a *nom de plume*, one that allowed Quilliam to give expression to his deepest personal thoughts and emotions at time of crisis. Moreover, amidst all his familiar didacticism, moralising and humour that can be found elsewhere in his poetic output, a strong inclination towards Sufism, both of the sober Junaydi *and* the more intoxicated Hallajian varieties also emerges. In lieu of a proper literary analysis, we only offer a couple of initial insights here.

The depth of Quilliam's sense of loss and longing for his daughter Habeeba who died in May 1908 from diphtheria at the tender age of eleven shines through *Sheikh Haroun Abdullah*. Firstly, the collection is dedicated "to my beloved daughter Habeeba in Paradise" (*SHA*, p.5). Then, in a complex way, Quilliam transposes his grief at the loss of his daughter on to "Sheikh Haroun" who is also similarly grief-stricken at the premature loss of his wife, also called Habeeba, in the poem, "*Essefler— Regrets*", (*SHA*, p.27), or anticipates meeting her again in paradise in "*Rāsikh Sev— Enduring Love*"

(*SHA*, p.28). Yet perhaps the "Habeeba" in this collection is also a stand-in for Quilliam's parting from his two wives, as he always worked on the volume away from England in Istanbul, as he states in the Preface. While the Introduction, with its very personal poetry attached directly to the biography of "Sheikh Haroun" was composed after the Young Turk Revolution in 1908 (as a *terminus post quem*), the bulk of poems is said to have been produced during various visits to Istanbul between 1903 and 1908 (*SHA*, p.11), although they may still have a *terminus ante quem* of 1914–16 too.

There are also possible allusions that show Quilliam making peace with himself after his years of crisis. For example, in "*Rijá—Entreaty*", he closes with what could be read as nostalgic sorrow for the loss of the Liverpool Muslim Institute:

> With opened eyes, I build, and then I see,
> The building dedicated unto Thee,
> Destroy'd, and yet 'twas beautiful to me.

Yet, elsewhere in "The Song That Lived", Quilliam chides himself for writing poems "to please the crowd" and for then compounding the error by writing "...to please the few;/His song was sung before a king/And then—became forgotten thing." Better he concludes to leave all thought of fame or honour:

> His inmost thoughts, then he did pen,
> Not caring he for king or men,
> He sang of joy, he spoke of tears,
> And lo! his song outliv'd the years.[32]

Along with Quilliam's more familiar "sober" moralising, the collection also shows yearning for God using a more intoxicated language of spiritual intimacy, e.g.: "I long to soar to Thee, to be with Thee above,/Thy Majesty o'erpowers, my heart yearns for Thy love." (p.33) There is also evidence of familiarity with Akbarian metaphysics, which suffuses the mystic poems, e.g. "That Allah all things made, and Allah made me too,/If made by Allah, then of Allah I am made, ... /With Allah e'er be, and be with Allah, One.", emphasising the unity of existence (*waḥdat al-wujūd*). Given Quilliam's reputation for sober Sufism, this adds another dimension to this complex religious personality, which deserves further examination. Indeed, our hope is that the establishment of this collection will stimulate greater public interest in his poetry, as well as encouraging further literary scholarship.

Acknowledgements

We would like to record our thanks to Abdurahman Abouhawas, Abdul Aziz Brown, Jamie Gilham, Riordan Macnamara, Münire Zeyneb Maksudoğlu, Brent Singleton, and the ever-helpful staff at the British Library Reading Rooms in Boston Spa for their assistance in obtaining the disparate primary sources needed to put this collection together; Mehmet Emin Gulecyuz, Timothy Winter, Michael Mumisa, and Omid Safi for lending us their expertise in early modern Ottoman, classical Arabic and classical Persian poetry; Christopher Starbuck for his initial suggestion that Sheikh Haroun Abdullah was yet another Quilliam pen-name; and Jamil Chishti and the team at Beacon Books for their editorial assistance and patient encouragement. Yahya would like to thank Fozia, Sulayman and Layla for their unending love and support in giving him the time and space to complete this project. Ron would like to, as always, thank Cathy and Dominic for their patience and sacrifice when he embarks on another project. He would also like to mention Yahya, who took the original conception of this collection and with untiring efforts made it into something much larger. Finally, any errors or omissions are our own, and we ask our dear readers to write to Beacon Books with any you spot so that we can correct future editions. True success only lies with Allah's pleasure and acceptance.

R & Y
Abercych and Ilkley
July 2021

Endnotes

1   For in-depth biographies and studies of Abdullah Quilliam see Ron Geaves, *Islam in Victorian Britain: The Life and Times of Abdullah Quilliam*. (Markfield: Kube, 2010); Ron Geaves and Gilham, Jamie (eds.), *Victorian Muslim: Abdullah Quilliam and Islam in the West*. (London: Hurst, 2017); Yusuf Samih Asmay, *Islam in Victorian Liverpool: An Ottoman Account of Britain's First Mosque Community* (Swansea: Claritas Books, 2021), trans. and eds. by Yahya Birt, Riordan Macnamara and Münire Zeyneb Maksudoğlu.

2   See Yahya Birt, "Islam in Liverpool: The Quilliams, Popular Conservatism and the New Trade Unionism in Liverpool", *The Islamic Review* (Special Edition), http://www.abdullahquilliam.org/wp-content/uploads/2018/12/Yahya-Birt-The-Quilliams-Popular-Conservatism.pdf visited 15th March 2019.

3   *Liverpool Weekly Courier*, 14th September 1901.

4   Corroboratory primary sources for Quilliam's Muslim Indian patrons are thin on the ground for the early 1890s, but one rare instance is 7000 rupees sent by Rangoon's Muslim businessmen for a mosque and a burial ground, see *Reis and Rayyet* (Calcutta), 9th January 1892, p.23. Thanks to Riordan Macnamara for the reference.

5   Geaves, *Islam in Victorian Britain*, p.61.

6   *Polly* (1891), *The Wages of Sin* (1894) and *King Bladud of Bath* (ca. 1900–4). The latter two were serialized in *The Crescent*.

7   See for example, Rosa Warren, described as "Longfellow by a Muslima", *TC*, Vol.VII, No.168, 1st April 1986, pp.630–1, 634–7; Stephen Nur-Uddin, "Some Poets and Prose Writers of Lancashire", *TC*, Vol.IX, No.211, 27th January 1897, pp.51–5, 58–9 and "A Sketch of English Literature", *TC*, Vol.XXVI, No.666, 18th October 1905, pp.243–7; Abdullah Quilliam, "The Boy Poet" writing about Thomas Chatterton in *TC*, Vol.IX, No.214, 17th February 1897, pp.101–3 and attributed to H. Mustapha Léon, "John Dryden, The Great English Poet", Vol.XXX, No.762, 25th August 1907, pp.131–5, 138–41.

8   Brent Singleton (ed.), *The Convert's Passion: An Anthology of Islamic Poetry from Late Victorian and Edwardian Britain* (USA: Borgo Press, 2009).

9   The editors hold different views about the status of Henri Mustapha Léon who wrote in *The Crescent* between 1897–1908. Ron takes the view he was a real person, a French medical doctor, LMI member and convert to Islam who received notices in *The Crescent* and the local press, while Yahya holds that it was a pen-name of Quilliam's that he often used to write about himself and other LMI members in the third person, which also nodded towards his second (then common-law) wife, Mary Lyon, and her five children, with the play on words (Lyon/Léon). In the 1901 Census, while maintaining a separate house for Mary and his family at 42 Rufford Rd, West Derby, he suggestively named himself as "Henry M. Quilliam, journalist and author". Three poems appear under this name, Henri Mustapha Léon, in *The Crescent*: "Victoria, In Memorium", *TC*, Vol.XVII, No.420, 30th January 1901, p.75; "The Terrible

Telephone", *TC*, Vol.XVIII, No.455, 2nd October 1901, p.221; "The Two Foes", *TC*, Vol.XVIII, No.589, 27th April 1904, p.266.

10 Blackburn: Geo. Toulmin & Sons for La Société Internationale de Philologie, Science et Beaux-Arts, 1916, 108pp. Toulmin & Sons was a regional publisher that mainly produced Lancashire newspapers, mostly notably the *Lancashire Daily Post*. In his *Who's Who* entries as H.M. Léon, mention is made of a collection of Turkish poems, *Bache* (*The Garden*), published in 1900, but it, along with two other Turkish titles, has never been found. In lieu of them being found, the suspicion remains that they were invented to pad out his bibliography before 1910, as they are not mentioned in his early *Who's Who* entries as W.H.A. Quilliam. For a comparison of the two entries, see the long footnote in Geaves, *Islam in Victorian Britain*, pp.335–7n26.

11 John Gross, *The Rise and Fall of the Man of Letters*. (New York: Macmillan, 1969).

12 Alister McGrath, *The Twilight of Atheism: The Rise and Fall of Disbelief in the Modern World*, (New York: Doubleday, 2004), p.53.

13 Alex Benchimol, *Intellectual Politics and Cultural Conflict in the Romantic Period: Scottish Whigs, English Radicals and the Making of the British Public Sphere* (London: Routledge, 2016).

14 Michael Scriven, *Hard Won Lessons in Program Evaluation*. (San Francisco: Jossey-Bass, 1993), p.119.

15 Geaves, *Islam in Victorian Britain*, p.20.

16 Quilliam objected to Leitner's restrictions on use of the Woking mosque for interfaith or inter-racial marriage, to promote political or religious causes or to proselytise Islam, see Geaves, *Islam in Victorian Britain*, pp.262–3.

17 Letter from R.W. Hall Caine to Dr Charles Poole, 10th January 1920, http:// quilliamandleon.blogspot.co.uk/, accessed 17th April 2018.

18 E.g. *The Era*, 16th April 1910, p.20; *The Stage*, 13th October 1910, p.19; *Daily Herald* (London), 1st February 1913, p.6. There are dozens of other brief notices and advertisements from these years that can form the basis of a skeleton timeline of this otherwise relatively blank period (1909–13) in Léon's life.

19 *Nottingham Evening Post*, 29th April 1932, p.10.

20 As was his habitual practice, Quilliam cited George Sale's 1734 translation of the Qur'an, which he modified where he thought it was incorrect. There is only one instance in this collection where he does not cite or modify Sale's translation.

21 *Maḥlaṣ*: A pen name, also called a *nom de plume* or a literary double, is a pseudonym adopted by an author and printed on the title page or by-line of their works in place of their real name.

22 Yahya Birt "Abdullah Quilliam and Sufism", *Medium*, 20th August 2016, https:// medium.com/@yahyabirt/abdullah-quilliam-and-sufism-1d17fa88f7c7, accessed 18th March 2020.

23 Aḥmad Tamīm'dārī, *The Book of Iran: A History of Persian Literature: Schools, Periods, Styles and Literary Genres* (UK: Alhoda UK, 2002), p.169.

24 Jean Boase Beier, "Poetry Translation" in Millan, C. and F. Bartrina (eds), *The Routledge Handbook of Translation Studies* (London: Routledge, 2012).

25 For use of all three pen-names in *The Philomath*: as Abdullah Quilliam, 1917, pp.52, 289; 1918, pp.16–17; as Léon, "translated from the Turkish", 1917, pp.14–15, 250; as well as ongoing promotion of the collection attributed to Sheikh Haroun Abdullah in the journal.

26 *Payghambar Ve Yahudi* (The Prophet and the Jew), *IR* (Woking), February 1915, p.73–4; *SHA*, pp.29, 57–8; *Acrimu-al-Hirrah!* (Respect the Cat!), *IR* (Woking), December 1914, pp.546–7; *SHA*, pp.29, 59–60; *Medh Peygamberin* (In Praise of the Prophet), *IR* (Woking), June 1915, p.286; *SHA*, p.81.

27 Esrâr Dede, *Tezkire-i Şu'arâ-yı Mevleviyye*, ed. İlhan Genç (Ankara: T.C. Kültür ve Turizm Bakanlığı, 2018); for a biography of Dede, see F. İz, "Esrar Dede", *EI2*, eds. P. Bearman et al (Leiden: Brill, 1954–2005). Neither is Sheikh Haroun Abdullah mentioned in E.J.W. Gibb, *A History of Ottoman Poetry* (London: Luzac & Co., 1900–9), 6 vols, a reference Quilliam quoted extensively in *The Crescent*, e.g. see his review of the fourth volume: *TC*, Vol.XXIX, No.735, 13th February 1907, p.941.

28 F. Babinger, "Nef'î" (980–1044H/1572–1635CE), *EI2*, Vol.8, p.3; F. İz, "Khayâlî", *EI2*, Vol.4, p.72; J.H. Kramers, "Münedjdjim Bashi", *EI2*, Vol.7, pp.572–3, Dede, *Tezkire*, p.29.

29 For example, Sultan Murad Khan IV's reign started in 1623 not 1631. Also there are oddities in the Turkish titles given to the poems if they are to match their English equivalents: "Rija Shairin" should be "Şairin Ricası"; "Ruzgar Sharhi" should be "Rüzgar Şarkısı"; "Uyqu ve Qardashani Ulum" should be "Uyku ve Kardeş-i Ulum"; "Sabah Yazı" should be "Yaz Sabahı"; and "Sev Hepsi Sev" should be either "Sev Hepsini Sev" ("Love, Love Them All"), or "Sev Hep Sev" ("Love, Always Love"), as Quilliam wrote.

30 O.M. Akün, "Divan Edebiyati", *DT İslâm Ansiklopedisi* (Istanbul: Türkiye Diyanet Vakfı, 1988–2016), 46 vols, https://islamansiklopedisi.org.tr/divan-edebiyati, accessed 9th March 2020; M.O. Okay, "Batililaşma", Section 5: Edebiyat, *DT İslâm Ansiklopedisi*; https://islamansiklopedisi.org.tr/batililasma#5-edebiyat, accessed 9th March 2020; Gibb, *History of Ottoman Poetry*; M.F. Köprülü, "'Othmānli", III—Literature, *EI2*, Vol.9, pp.210–21.

31 Although John (Yehya-en-Nasr) Parkinson's review of *SHA* can be read as straightforwardly positive, see *Asiatic Review*, Vol.IX, No.25, July 1916 pp.100–1, his aside near the start of it could also be read as evidence that, as an old friend and colleague, he was in on the act, it being a possible allusion to Sheikh Haroun Abdullah as a pen-name (*maḫlaṣ*) for Léon/Quilliam: "the translations of his poems have been so admirably rendered that the reader might well mistake them for original poetic effusions in English" (p.100).

32 *TP*, 1917, p.52.

Part I

Collected Poems
(1892–1926)

MOSLEM MORNING HYMN

Regularly perform the prayer at daybreak, for the prayer is borne witness unto by angels.... And say, O Lord, cause me to enter with a favourable entry, and cause me to come forth with a favourable coming forth; and grant me from Thee an assisting power. Sura 17, Koran.[1]

Oh Allah, for another night
    Of peaceful sleep and rest,
For all the joys of morning light,
    Be Thou for ever blest.
Here on this new born day we give
    Ourselves anew to Thee;
That as Thou wishest we may live,
    And what Thou willest be.

Favour us with Thy blessing, God,
    As we this day begin;
Preserve us from all evil, Lord,
    And keep us free from sin.
Assist us by Thy mighty power;
    Thy helping aid us lend,
To serve Thee from this early hour
    Until the day shall end.

Whate'er we do, great things or small,
    Whate'er we speak or think;
Thy glory may we seek in all,
    And from no duty shrink.
Merciful God, to Thee we pray
    Us to protect and bless,
And keep us by Thy grace alway[2]
    In paths of righteousness.[3]

---

1   Modification of Sale, 17:78 (partial), 17:80, p.280.
2   An archaic form of always.
3   *Hymns*, p.1; reproduced in *The Moslem World* (New York), Vol.I, No.1, May 1893, p.7; *AR*, Vol.4, No.3, July 1893, p.7. This is the first hymn in the collection, numbered No.1 and is marked as being "L.M.", Long Metre or 88.88 (four lines of eight syllables) and signed as W.H. Quilliam.

UNTITLED (1892A)

*By the brightness of the morning; and by the night, when it groweth dark; thy
Lord hath not forsaken thee.* Sura 63, Koran.[1]

Oh, True believers now rejoice
    And be your praises loud and long,
Let every heart and every voice
    Conspire to raise a joyful song.

Loud let your anthem rise to God,
    Whose favouring mercies so abound;
Swift let His praises fly abroad,
    The circuit of the earth around.

The brightness of the morning light
    Which every day brings back to thee,
The growing darkness of the night,
    And signs of His great majesty.

Then praise Him who gavest thee life,
    And to your mind this comfort be,
That though this world be full of strife,
    Thy Lord hath not forsaken thee.[2]

1   Sale, 93:1–3, p.583.
2   *Hymns*, p.5. In Long Metre, and No.4 in the collection, signed as W.H. Quilliam.

UNTITLED (1892B)

Celebrate the praise of God. Sura 110, Koran.[1]

Come let us sing praises to God,
     Whom all our fathers knew;
And walk according to his word,
     Revealed by prophets true.

To man was first given the law,
     When placed in Eden's bowers;
And if we the true God adore,
     Precious rewards are ours.

The holy prophet Abram too,
     Whose name we all revere,
Worshipped the only One and true,
     Who doth for aye endure.

And Noah inspir'd by the Lord,
     To all did preach and say,
O worship the only true God
     And leave your sinful way.

But they shut their ears to his call,
     And His words did deride;
And the flood destroyed them all
     Who thus God had defied.

Then Moses with manifest power
     Was sent at God's command,
And he, at the appointed hour,
     Led forth the chosen band.

---

1   Sale, 110:3, p.594.

And David, the prophet and king,
    Upon his royal seat,
Praises to God did daily sing,
    In psalms and hymns so sweet.

Jesus and Mahomet also,
    Ascribed to Him all praise;
Then let us to God's temple go,
    And our glad voices raise.

And sing with heart and cheerful voice
    And thank Him while we've breath,
And from our birth in Him rejoice,
    Until the day of death.[2]

---

2   *Hymns*, pp.8–9. In Common Metre (86.86), and No.8 in the collection, signed as W.H.
    Quilliam.

JUMMA HYMN

Whoever striveth to promote the true religion, striveth for the advantage of his own soul.[1]

Once more within these sacred walls,
    Let us our hearts and voices raise,
And bless great Allah, Lord of all,
    With notes of joy, and songs of praise.

Our worldly thoughts now put aside,
    Our foolish fears and doubts dispel,
For if we in Allah confide,
    He'll surely guide our footsteps well.

Weak is our strength, small is our power,
    Our good resolves, how soon they fall;
But God we know is our strong tower,
    And keepeth those who heed His call.

Then let us now ourselves anew,
    To Him alone now dedicate;
And soon our Allah we shall view,
    And dwell within the heav'nly gate.[2]

---

1   Sale, 29:6 (partial), p.388.
2   *Hymns*, p.18. In Long Metre, No.21 in the collection, and signed as W.H. Quilliam.

THE MOSLEM'S HAVEN OF REFUGE

For those who believe, and do that which is right, are destined gardens beneath which rivers flow; this shall be great felicity. Sura 85.[1]

What though misfortune's adverse cares
Calumny's dark and coward snares,
And poverty's chill wave,
Should all against weak man combine,
To blast him e'en at wisdom's shrine,
And drag him to the grave!

What though the Moslem's heart be torn
By persecutions rankling thorn,
While traversing earth's vale;
Though even life's career he ends.
While no lov'd object o'er him bends
To catch his parting tale!

Yet is there not a bourne on high,
Where happiness can never die
Beneath extinction's rod!
Where blessed peace for ever reigns
Where love calls music with her strains
To hymn the living God!

Where virtue, freed from mortal clay
Ecstatic, does for ever stay
Through all the countless days?
Where world-illuming suns enshine,
Regions ethereal, pure, divine,
Declare great Allah's praise.

---

1   Sale, 85:11, p.576.

Then ne'er let fragile man despair,
Though throbs his burning brow with care,
His bosom though oppress'd
But let his musing visions soar
To that eternal hallow'd shore,
Where is eternal rest.[2]

2   *Hymns*, pp.31–2. In 886.886, a form of long metre in hymnody. No.35 in the collection, and
    signed as W.H. Quilliam. Written on the evening of 15 November 1891, immediately after a
    violent attack on the mosque while the Liverpool Muslims were praying Maghrib "Nimaz"; also
    published in *AR*, Vol.3, No.2, February 1892, p.16; here signed as W.H.A. Quilliam.

THE FIRST SURA PARAPHRASED

Praise be to God the Lord of all creatures. Sura 1, Koran.[1]

Praise be to God the Lord of all,
    Praise Him all creatures great and small;
With raptures now, the mercies sing,
    Of Him the day of judgment's King.

Exclaim, O Lord, we worship Thee,
    Now while we kneel on bended knee;
Oh grant us by Thy mighty power,
    Needful assistance every hour.

Direct us Lord in the right way,
    Nor ever let us go astray;
Graciously keep us in Thy path,
    Preserve us from Thy holy wrath.

And when the sands of life have run,
    And all our time on earth be done;
We pray Thee O Thou God of love,
    Take us to Thee in heaven above.[2]

---

1   Sale, 1:1, p.1. Here is a prime example of Quilliam's Anglo Islamic-Christian syncretism, taking the subject matter of the opening chapter of the Qur'an, rewriting it as a long-metre hymn that was sung, accompanied by an organist.
2   *Hymns*, p.37. In Long Metre, No.42 in the collection, signed as W.H. Quilliam.

UNTITLED (1892C)

God ordereth all things. Sura 15, Koran.
How happy shall the companions of the right hand be. Sura 56, Koran.[1]

Almighty Allah, Lord of all,
Former of this terrestrial ball,
Who gavest the sun, to shine by day,
The night illumn'd by moon's bright ray;
Teach us to walk in the right way,
All Thy holy commands obey.

Thee we adore, we own Thy power,
Thy aid we need each passing hour,
Thy bounty clothes with plants the ground,
And scatters mercies all around;
Keep us from evil, e'en as far
As earth from the most distant star.

Ruler of all, whose wise decree
Has fixed the limits of the sea,
Upon the land form'd hills and plains,
Who sendest the refreshing rains;
Watch o'er us still where e'er we be,
And from all evil keep us free.

O God, who raised the heavens on high,
Sprinkled with stars at night the sky,
Whose power hath stretched forth the earth,
To whom all creatures owe their birth;
Teach us to act, now while we've breath
Always to be prepared for death.

---

1   Sale, 56:8 (partial), p.516. The first citation is not in the 15th chapter.

That so when all our time is o'er,
And life to us shall be no more,
When earth and stars have passed away,
And has arrived the judgment day,
That we, O Allah, then may stand
Companions there of Thy right hand.[2]

---

2   *Hymns*, pp.42–3. In 8.8.8.8.8.8., form of long metre in hymnody. No.49 in the collection, signed as W.H. Quilliam.

AN ISHA PRAYER[1]

God grant Thy servants peace,
And blessings still increase
    Upon us here.
To us Thy will unfold,
In grace us still behold;
    Our weary spirits cheer
With peaceful thoughts.

Bless us and all at home;
Protect all those that roam
    From sin and death.
Now night returns again
Let us in peace remain,
    And guard our every breath
Till morning light.[2]

---

1   Evening prayer.
2   *IW*, Vol.I, No.2, June 1893, p.17; *TC*, Vol.IX, No.232, 23rd June 1897, p.397.

IN MEMORIAM

William Obeid-Ullah Cunliffe[1]
Died Sunday, 24th February 1894
"God inviteth you unto the dwelling of peace." Sura 10, Jonas, Koran.[2]

Gone from this world of sorrow,
Gone from its toils and tears,
Gone to that bright to-morrow,
To rest through endless years.

Now all his cares are ended,
Now all his labour is done,
His soul above descended,
To receive the prize it won.

He died without even a struggle,
Or convulsive throb of the breast,
He was leaving this world of trouble,
And entering eternal rest.

The clay form that encircled his spirit,
While here on this earth he abode,
Has released the soul that did merit,
And receives now reward from God.

His name will be treasured for ever,
Whenever Islam shall be taught,
As one whose every endeavour
Was to act as a Muslim ought.

Then let each Muslim stand by each other,
And, praying to Allah so true,
Beseech that the seed sown by our brother
May yield a full harvest true.

---

1   Obeid-Ullah Cunliffe (ca. 1831–94) was a London-based engineer, who converted to Islam in
    1892. He contributed at least 15 poems to Quilliam's publications in his two short years as a
    Muslim before his death.
2   Sale, 10:25 (partial), p.242.

That England may soon be reclaimed
From its present bigoted creed,
And follow the teachings of Ahmed,
God's prophet in truth and in deed.[3]

3   Originally published in *IW*, March 1894, Vol.I, No.11, p.32.

THE MOSLEM'S REFUGE

The 113th and 114th Suras rendered into English Verse

While slowly fade the glorious beams of light,
And around me gather now the shades of night,
While Earth is wrapt in deep obscurity,
Refuge, O Lord, I only have in Thee.

When plotting men arrange their deep-laid schemes
With craft and art, unthought of e'en in dreams,
From their vile plans thus laid so cunningly,
Refuge, O Lord, I only have in Thee.

In tangled forests, lost and far from home,
In distant lands, if perchance I should roam,
When wild and furious beasts roar savagely,
Refuge, O Lord, I only have in Thee.

When storms and winds arise, and tempests lower,
And crashing peals of thunder show their power,
And direful lightning flashes vividly,
Refuge, O Lord, I only have in Thee.

When weakened pulse, and still more feeble breath,
Betokes the time when o'er bridge of death
I leave this world to meet Eternity,
Refuge, O Lord, I only have in Thee.[1]

1   *IW*, Vol.II, No.15, July 1894, p.95; *AR*, Vol.3, No.9, September 1892, p.108, signed as W.H.
    Abdullah Quilliam, with some slight changes in wording and reordering of the stanzas, and titled
    as "The Daybreak", with the subtitle "The 113th Sura Rendered Into English Verse".

ABU-BEKR'S ORATION AFTER
THE DEATH OF THE PROPHET

From The Crescent

Weep, Mecca, weep, Thy Son is slain!
Who, dauntless, freedom's battles fought,
And with heroic courage sought
Thy highest welfare and Thy gain.
Let jewelled tears of love bedew
The spot that bosoms him to rest;
Whilst in our hearts, his memory blest
With flowers of honour we bestrew.
His massive nobleness of mould
Most manly beauty did enfold;
A gorgeous place—Nature's best,
She gave it to her favour'd guest,
In whom were blended strength and grace,
And sunshine ever in his face.
The sculptor's eye in him would scan,
God's model of a perfect man.
This nobleness of outward mien
Was but the image of his mind,
So great, so noble, and so kind:
Thus Nature makes the unseen seen.
His soul turned artist, and did trace
Upon their earthen vessel, fair,
In beauteous lines and figures rare
Its own sweet picture: noble face.
Instinct with freedom, hating cant,
The throne of Lies he would Supplant.
Oppression's mighty chains, he broke,
King Sham sat trembling when he spoke.
With satire's shafts he pierced the heart
Of falseness with its wily art,
The Traitor's meanness he withstood
But loved the guiltless, true, and good
His mind, gigantic in its might,
Made vexing problems yield reply;
Perplexities could not defy

The keenness of his mental sight.
And as intrepid diver brings
The pearls from ocean caverns deep,
So, also, Nature could not keep
From him her hidden precious things.
Like water bubbling from some springs,
His wit came sparkling with clear ring;
His thoughts were oft, in humour dressed
To gladden minds that were depressed;
And oftentimes his words would flow
In tend'rest pathos sweet and low;
Such words, like those from heaven above,
To sorrowing souls brought peace and love.
His heart was like the ocean vast,
That stretches out its bosom wide,
On which the stately ships do ride,
With flying banners from their mast;
But ne'er did treach'rous storm arise,
As sometimes happens on the sea,
He bore all's burdens tenderly,
And ever sunny were his skies.
His public utterance, like a flame
Burden abuses and their shame;
But milder themes would always prove
His lips were touched with grace and love.
What pow'r of Eloquence he had!
Who moved us from the gay to sad,
Or sad to gay, as he deemed fit,
With pathos pow'r or pow'r of wit.
The tongue of Eloquence is stilled,
Which our poor souls with raptures filled;
The sympathetic heart lies cold,
And thus is all Life's story told.
'Tis false, 'tis false—It is not true.
In death, True Life begins anew;
Though to the grave we all must come,
Beyond that grave we find our home.[1]

---

1   Signed as W.H. Abdullah Quilliam, *AR*, Vol.5, No.3, July 1894, pp.12–13, taken from the
     currently missing volume of *The Crescent* from 1894. Here a eulogy is assigned to the Prophet's

SCALE FORCE

*God is the creator of all things; He is the one, the victorious God. He causeth
water to descend from heaven, and the brooks flow according to their
respective measure, and the floods bear the flowing froth.* Sura 13, Ar Rad
(Thunder), Koran.[1]

It falls
Within a rift between the granite walls,
On either side, the bleak cold stone
Where leafy ferns, and tender moss alone
Find resting-place. Between the waving shrubs on high,
Calm and serene, is dimly seen the sky.
Whilst down the narrow gorge the stream
In one long, silvery thread doth seem,
In one continual glittering shower,
An avalanche of diamonds to outpour.
Beneath the fall, a cup-like bowl
Receives the stream, then onward it doth roll,
With a low rumbling, grumbling sound,
O'er ruddy boulders, now worn smooth and round
Until another smaller leap it takes,
While all around the spray, like snowy flakes,
Is scattered. Then, as though its mighty wrath
Had been in one great angry burst poured forth,
It gently ripples through the grassy mead,
And to the distant lake doth slowly speed,
And seems as though it murmured on its road
Low cadences of hymns to Nature's God,
Whose mighty power hath formed them all,
The brook, the lake, the rocks, and waterfall.[2]

---

close Companion, Abu Bakr, that in fact constitutes Quilliam's first poem in praise of the
Prophet.

1 Sale, 13:16–17 (partial), p.242.
2 *TC*, Vol.5, No.104, 9th January 1895, p.14; *TC*, Vol.XXVII, No.677, 3rd January 1906, p.11.
Scale Force, near Buttermere, is the highest waterfall in the English Lake District, and located in
a deep gorge on the northern flank of Red Pike. The poem reveals his awareness of the Romantic
poets, especially Wordsworth.

THE TRIUMPH OF TRUTH

Truth is come, and falsehood is vanished,
and shall not return any more. Sura 34, Saba, Koran.[1]

The thrones of time shall pass away,
    As Egypt, Babylon and Tyre;
Earth's mighty cities all decay,
    And kings and conquerors expire;
But Truth shall, in eternal bloom,
    Survive, though unbelievers rage.
Shall see foul error meets its doom
    And flourish through eternal age.

The sun may cease to pour forth light,
    And lost may be moon's silv'ry ray,
The stars expire in endless night,
    Vanish the planets all away,
But Truth shall raise her peerless head
    Above the ruins of them all;
And smile, when time and tide are fled,
    Before the Truth falsehood shall fall.

Exultant then shall be the cry
    O'er error's throne, prostrate in dust,
And Muslims see that God, Most High,
    In whom they always put their trust,
Bid Truth begin its endless reign,
    Falsehood vanquish'd and triumph'd o'er,
The "True Direction" made most plain,
    And error to return no more.[2]

---

1   Sale, 34:49 (partial), p.425.
2   It was written on the 22nd December 1894 and published in *IW*, Vol.II, No.21, January 1895,
    p.263; *TC*, Vol.5, No.108, 6th February 1895, p.48.

THE LESSONS OF EXPERIENCE

How bright the untried future seemed,
When years ago I sat and dreamed,
    In youth's sweet morning hours,
With not a thought of weary pain,
Which riper years bring in their train,
    To blight hope's fairest flowers.

With eager eyes, yet half afraid,
I scanned the time then just ahead;
    When joyous boyhood o'er,
School-days expired, tasks thrown aside,
My little barque borne on life's tide
    Would unknown shores explore.

These years rolled on; I then attained
My full manhood; the heights were gained,
    Which once seemed far away;
Did hopes in full fruition lie?
No; they were only born to die—
    Frail blossoms of a day.

And I have learn'd that human life
Is one of pain, of care, and strife;
    That only now and then
Bright sunbeams o'er our path will stray
To cheer awhile our gloomy way,
    Then quickly fade again.

Yet still this lesson I've been taught,
Although I've not gain'd all I sought,
    And pride's had many a fall,
Yet to freely say, with mind unsoiled,
'Tis better to have liv'd and toiled
    Than never liv'd at all.[1]

---

1   *TC*, 30th January 1895, Vol.V, No.107, p.34. It was written on 26th January 1896.

Invite men unto the way of thy Lord, by wisdom and mild exhortation, and disfute with them in the most condescending manner; for thy Lord well knoweth him who strayeth from His path, and he well knoweth those who are rightly directed. Sura 16, The Bee, Koran.[1]

Be not hasty in opinion;
    Slowly judge your fellow men;
Haste may hide the good dominion
    Acts of folly have outran;
What if he has erred often,
    Should we not remember still
Gentle admonitions soften
    And attract the stubborn will?
Language harsh and wanting feeling
    Bow the spirit for a time,
Rankles where the wound was healing,
    And perhaps excites to crime.

Are you free from human errors?
    Are your faults so few to scan
That you wield a sword of terrors
    O'er your weaker fellow man?
Lift the veil from that proud spirit,
    Ask if you remember aught
Where loud censure you did merit
    Had you then been fairly caught?
Every man should guard his station
    And his failings fairly scan,
And remember that temptation
    Comes to all his fellow man.[2]

---

1   Sale, 16:125, p.270. Referring here to the older sense of condescending, i.e. to give up one's rights or claims, to consent, to agree, or to acquiesce, instead of today's primary sense, which is to patronize someone regarded as a social inferior. See *OED*, "Condescend".
2   Written 21st March 1895 and published in *TC*, Vol.V, No.116, 27th March 1895, p.99.

CIRCUMSTANCES ALTER CASES

Inquire not too curiously into other men's failings. Sura 49, Koran.[1]

A rich man proudly walked along
    The straight and narrow way;
He lifted up his head in pride
    To hear the people say:
"That is a pure and honest man—
    The noblest work of God;
He is built upon a perfect plan,
    He virtue's path has trod."

"No moral law does he transgress,
    He's good and true and kind;
'Tis hard amongst the walks of man
    A purer soul to find."
'Twas thus they praised him while he lived,
    And filled his heart with pride,
And when at last his end did come,
    And like the rest he died.

The priest, above his gilded bier,
    Exalted to the skies
The soul of this proud child of wealth
    As good, as great, and wise.
And said that straight to heaven's gate
    The rich man's soul was sent
While all the people bowed, and said
    "To paradise he went."

---

1   Sale, 49:12, p.498.

A poor man with his load of grief
    Went staggering down the path,
And begged of God to grant relief
    And heap not on him wrath.
With weight of many grievous fears
    He tottered o'er the road,
And called on Allah thro' his tears
    To add not to his load.

He fell upon the wayside sore,
    And yielded unto sin,
And he the law, with iron hand,
    To prison, quick dragg'd in.
The cold, stern judge said, with a frown,
    "A crime thou didst commit,
And thou in bond must now be kept
    Till thou hast answered it."

Into a dungeon, dark and lone,
    The poor man straight they sent,
And chained him to the prison wall,
    And bade him there repent.
And there for years he pined away,
    No loved one by his side,
Until a fairer fortune came,
    And then the poor man died.

No prayers above his cold, dumb clay,
    The silk-clad Bishop said;
But quick they bore his form away,
    As soon as he was dead.
No tears were shed above his grave,
    No mound above it rais'd;
Neglected and despised he lived—
    He died despised, unprais'd.

But had he lived 'neath brighter stars,
     Perhaps the narrow way
His feet on earth had gladly trod,
     That went so far astray.
And had the rich man felt the weight
     Of care the other bore.
He might have fallen by the way,
     As men have done before.[2]

2   Written 29th January 1895 and published in *IW*, Vol.II, No.24, April 1895, pp.373–4; *TC*, Vol.V, No.123, 22nd May 1895, p.163.

THOUGHTS FOR THINKERS

Wealth and children are the ornament of this present life; but good works, which are permanent, are better in the sight of thy Lord, with respect to the reward, and better with respect to hope. Sura 18, The Cave, Koran.[1]

Oh! Brethren, it is well to know,
  As on celestial things you ponder,
That wealth and honours here below
  Are counted as but naught up yonder.

To adverse fortune meekly bow,
  In Allah's mercy still confide,
For, though wretched your fortunes now,
  You yet in heaven may abide.

A monarch may ascend the throne
  With all desire to rule aright,
And lay the regal symbol down,
  To wear above a crown of light.

Not titled earls, nor crowned kings,
  As such, are recognised above;
Kind deeds and words and other things—
  There merit rank and perfect love.

Our good deeds are sweet thoughts sublime,
  Made manifest, and starlike shine,
Recorded there from time to time
  By angels in a book divine.

Thus time may show with glory fraught,
  Some humble, good, retiring soul,
Who wealth and honours never sought,
  The most exalted of the whole.[2]

---

1   Sale, 18:46, pp.289–90.
2   *TC*, Vol.V, No.118, 17th April 1895, p.121.

WHICH OF THEM WAS NEIGHBOUR UNTO HER?

"Alas! For the rarity
Of Christian charity
Under the sun!"[1]

I saw a woman beg in the street
On the Christmas day, for bread to eat;
And loud the church-bells were chiming then,
The refrain of "peace and good will to men."

I saw a Christian, sleek and well-fed,
Pass the woman and turn his head;
The crumbs that under his table fell
That day, would have fed the beggar well.

Following the Christian churchman came
A woman whose brow was stamp'd with shame;
Out from her purse, a coin she cast,
And the beggar bless'd her, as she pass'd.

To the church the sleek man went his way;
The woman of shame, she blush'd to pray;
Yet which of them, more blest will be
Magdalene scorn'd, or proud Pharisee?[2]

---

1 Quotation from the famous poem "The Bridge of Sighs" written in 1844 by Thomas Hood. The poem was inspired by the suicide of a homeless young woman who threw herself from Waterloo Bridge on the Thames in London.
2 Written 26th December 1894 and published in *TC*, Vol.V, No.120, 1st May 1895, p.187.

TO A CHILD PLAYING WITH TOY BRICKS

Lay the blocks on nice and even,
    Place them skillfully with care;
Then your mimic house will grow, love,
    Strong and high, and very fair.

Little Florrie's eyes are gazing
    At the walls as they uprise;
"What a lovely house, dear Henry
    You have built," she gaily cries.

Still be patient, little builder—
Haste will but your work undo;
If the walls fall down before you,
    Other walls have fallen too.

Older hands have oft erected
    Larger castles far than thine,
Built in hope and expectation,
    Yet they crumble and decline.

Waste no time in weeping vainly
    Over errors you have made.
Work again and build still stronger,
    Someday you will be repaid.[1]

---

1   *IW*, Vol.III, No.25, May 1895, p.9; *TC*, Vol.V, No.126, 12th June 1895, p.190. A typical
    example of Victorian moral poetry of the period.

TRUE PLEASURES

How sweet to rove at opening day,
  When May's choice flow'rs are springing;
To feel the morning's early ray,
  And hear the warblers singing.

How sweet to rest in shady grove,
  When summer sun is shining;
And watch within the gay alcove,
  The tendrils gently twining.

Those happy moments, Oh! How sweet,
  When true love's vows are plighted;
And all the hopes and wishes meet,
  In heart and soul united!

Sweet, then, is the responsive sigh,
  From maiden's bosom stealing;
Sweet too, the pledge and tender tie,
  The fond affection sealing.

How sweet is liberty to those
  In dungeons dark and dreary;
And sweet the hour of calm repose,
  To pilgrims weak and weary.

And Oh! How doubly sweet it be,
  The joy that follows mourning;
And, for a parent, sweet to see
  A long-lost child returning.

Sweet, too, is friendship's soothing balm,
  With tender, kind, emotion;
But sweeter far the holy calm
  Of Islamic devotion!

When fervent strains of gratitude,
    Breath'd from a heart o'erflowing,
Ascend to God, who ev'ry good
    So richly is bestowing.

To stand within the Muslim zone,
    Each brother kindly greeted,
And feel 'tis not from lips alone
    Ul Humdo[1] is repeated.[2]

---

1   An eccentric rendering of *Alhamdulillah* (praise be to God), sometimes translated as "thank God" (J.M. Cowan (ed.) *The Hans Wehr Dictionary of Modern Written Arabic* (3rd edn., 1979), p.204. It is frequently invoked by Muslims and appears for the first time in the opening verse of the Qur'an.

2   Written 1ˢᵗ May 1895 and published in *IW*, Vol.III, No.26, June 1895, p.64; *TC*, Vol.VI, No.133, 31ˢᵗ July 1895, p.75.

THE SONG OF THE GOLDEN GORSE

Ellan Vannin veg veen—There is always gold on cushags there. Manx Saying.

I tell you I'm Queen of the Mountain.
    I feel a spoilt beauty's pride
As I peer from the reed-lined fountain,
    The gem of the waterside.
By the side of the running waters,
    With glorious golden sheen
Do I of Fair Mona's daughters
    Long reign as the Mountain Queen?

The glen and the ravine adorning,
    High up on some rocky ledge;
Your efforts to reach me, I scorning,
    Cling close to its moss-bound edge
In a palace of Nature's building,
    My throne on the scarped cliff keen,
Like the sun beams, its side bright gilding,
    Of reign as the Mountain Queen.

From my mountain home you would tear me,
    For her whose fond love you prize:
Nor less is the love you bear me,
    In kindling of her bright eyes.
But whether by stream or in bower,
    Or Manx maid's bosom seen,
You call me the best, brightest flower,
    And say I'm the Mountain Queen.

When the raging torrents of winter
    Rush madly over my head,
But deeper my roots will then enter,
    And grow in their turfy bed,
Till summer's bright sunshine returning
    To me a new life will mean,
And then you once more will be yearning
    To capture the Mountain Queen.[1]

---

1   *TC*, Vol.VI, No.131, 17ᵗʰ July 1895, p.44; *The Manxman*, 27ᵗʰ July 1895, p.11; the first
    two stanzas were republished in *TC*, Vol.XI, No.266, 16ᵗʰ February 1898, p.103. The first
    of Quilliam's poems inspired by his family's origins on the Isle of Man. Quilliam may have
    been referring to the Island's highest peak named "Snaefell", Norse for "Snow Mountain".
    Wordsworth visited in 1833 and wrote a series of sonnets which included references to the peak.

ODE TO ELLAN VANNIN[1]

Beauteous are thy rising hills
And the gently murmuring rills
Flowing through thy meads so green,
Oh how charming is the scene!
Let me have a cot beside
Mona's gently flowing tide;
Where, along its pebbly strand
Oft at evening would I stand,
While the trembling moonbeams pale
Quiver o'er each hill and dale.
This sweet season would I choose
And I'd court the passive muse,
But when winter's icy blast
O'er each mount and vale is cast,
To my home I'd then retreat,
By the cheering fireside seat;
There with Byron I'd converse,
Or great Shakespeare's muse rehearse;
And when comes the bloom of night
And its nobler themes invite,
Then with Orry[2] I can stray
O'er that lovely milky way;
View each planet in its sphere,
Rolling through the passing year.
Thus amusement I will find,
Quite enough for thoughtful mind;
These all point the certain road
To the throne of Nature's God.[3]

1   The name for the Isle of Man in the Manx language. *Ellan Vannin* is also a poem and song, often
     referred to as "the alternative Manx national anthem", written by Eliza Craven Green in 1854. Is
     Quilliam attempting his own anthem for the island he loved so much?
2   King Orry, an almost legendary figure revered as the greatest king and founder of the Crovan
     dynasty that ruled the island for two centuries. He is credited with the introduction of the
     island's legal system.
3   *TC*, Vol.VII, No.162, 19th February 1896, p.531; *TC*, Vol.XXI, No.528, 25th February 1903,
     p.115, where it is retitled "Ode to Manxland".

HOPE ON! HOPE EVER!

Wherefore persevere with patience; for the prosperous issue shall attend the pious. Sura 11, Hud, Koran.[1]

Shed no tears when the dark skies frown,
    Patiently rest;
No storm the rainbow's smile can drown;
    Hope for the best!

Still there's a light somewhere; some day
    From East to West
Will shine a deathless, glorious ray—
    Hope for the best!

Old adage! Yes, but not less sweet,
    Divinely blest!
Although the sharp stones gash your feet,
    Hope for the best!

What good is sighing? The time yet flies,
    Life is unrest;
Blot not the blue in Allah's skies,
    Hope for the best!

'Tis not the dross, but sterling gold
    That stands the test.
Pursue with patience, firmly hold—
    Hope for the best!

Hope on! Hope ever! You will find
    Your life-long quest
Peace for the soul, calm for the mind,
    Eternal rest.[2]

---

1   Sale, 11:49, p.216.
2   *TC*, Vol.VII, No.166, 18th March 1896, p.606.

A GEM FROM SAADI

Bamedadan ki lafawt nekuned layl u nehar.
Khosh burved dameni sahraa vou tamesha ye behar.
Sofi ez sauxmia ger Khaima bezed ber gubzar.
Kin ni vakt ist ki der Khané nishinee beekar.[1]

Saadi

When night and day in length are equal,
And the grass springs from the sod,
From admiring nature comes the sequel
Of admiring Nature's God.

This is no time for mourning,
Come out in the sunlight,
And humbly adoring God,
In all His works delight.[2]

---

1   Sa'di, *Kolliyat-e Sa'di*, ed. M.A. Foroughi and B. Khorramshahi (Tehran: Nahid, 1386H/2007CE),
    pp.662–3, cited and translated by Domenico Ingenito, *Beholding Beauty: Sa'di of Shiraz
    and the Aesthetics of Desire in Medieval Persian Poetry* (Leiden: Brill, 2021), p.289. Ingenito
    describes Sa'di's *qasida* (poem of praise) as "a lyrical observation of nature during springtime" in
    contemplation of the Qur'anic command to behold and marvel at what is in the heavens and the
    earth (10:101). The more faithful rendering by Ingenito shows that the translation offered above
    is very loose:
    > At dawn, when one can discern no difference between day and night,
    > How beautiful appear the edges of the valleys and the vision of springtime.
    > Tell the Sufi to leave the monastery and settle amidst the garden of roses
    > As this is not the time for one to sit idle at home!

2   Published in *TC*, Vol.VII, No.170, 8th April 1896, p.653.

A MUSLIM PRAYER

Oh, Allah! Lead me onward,
    Nor let my footsteps fall,
While marching to the graveside,
    That waiteth there for all.

Smooth Thou the rugged pathway,
    That leads towards the goal,
To which each pious Muslim,
    Directs his heart and soul.

Protect me when in danger,
    In sorrow comfort give,
Al-Hafiz! God Preserver!
    It is by Thee we live.

And when my life be over,
    And all my race is run,
Al-Jannat be my portion
    Al-Latif, Gracious One![1]

---

1   Written 24th December 1895 and published in *TC*, Vol.VII, No.175, 20th May 1896, p.743.

SONG OF THE EGYPTIAN WAR
(TRANSLATED FROM THE FRENCH)

Arise, O race once warlike,
  Why sleep ye on the ground?
Cast off this profound slumber
  In which ye now are found.

Wearied by long enslavement,
  Old Nile, as if in pain
Humbled in its abasement,
  Drags wearily its shame.

List to the sound now breaking.
  It is the rising wave
That soon will snap the fetters
  And free the weary slave.

O Muezzin, with your strong voice,
  From minaret's tall height
Call to their arms and duty
  Each turban-bearing knight.

I see from the pyramids
  Five thousand giants tall—
Egyptians, Turks and Seljukees—
  They stand a compact wall.

March forward now to victory,
  Flashing your weapons good!
Restore your ancient glory
  With the invader's blood.

From seaboard unto Nubia—
  Where'er the sun doth shine—
Fight like avenging heroes
  Until the land be thine.

Come in quick sailing wherries
    From all parts hereabouts
Swear to expel these boasters
    Before your marabouts.

Raise the standard of the Prophet,
    Which longs to see the light!
Before it e'en these English
    Will tremble with afright.

This time all our graveyards
    With all their bodies shall be filled;
Tel-el-Kabir be our conquest
    Lo! This has Allah willed.[1]

---

1   Another translation, this time from French but Quilliam does not reveal his source. Published
in *TC*, Vol.VII, No.180, 24th June 1896, p.830. The poem refers to the British Conquest of
Egypt, also known as Anglo–Egyptian War, which had occurred in 1882 between Egyptian
and Sudanese forces and the United Kingdom. It ended the nationalist uprising against the
Khedive Tewfik Pasha. It established complete British influence over Egypt at the expense of the
Egyptians, the French and the Ottomans, although they had nominal authority. Quilliam would
oppose British foreign policy and intervention in Ottoman affairs.

HYMN FOR THE PROPHET'S BIRTHDAY

The people that in darkness sat
    A glorious light have seen
God's prophet now to them has come—
    Muhammad, Al-Emin!

We hail thee, Allah's prophet true,
    Of prophecy the seal!
We read with reverence the book
    Thou wast sent to reveal.

For thou the burden dids't remove,
    Idolatry's fell rod;
In thy day the idols fall
    Before the sword of God.

To bless Arabia and the world
    Most surely thou wast raised;
We'll sing thy praises evermore,
    Our Mustapha, the praised.

We watch with gentle, fostering care,
    The seed that thou hast sown;
And trust to hear the world declare
    "La Allah," God is One.[1]

---

1   Quilliam adds a note that this hymn is so arranged that it can be sung to "Horsley" or any common metre tune. It is one of the many hymns that he adapted from the English Hymnal to be Islamically correct while using commonly known tunes. Note also that it is the first poem to be dated in the Islamic calendar. Written 1ˢᵗ Rabi' al-Awwal, 1314 and published in *TC*, Vol. VIII, No.187, 12ᵗʰ August 1896, p.941.

Two little blue eyes
    Peering at mine,
Gazing so tenderly,
    Almost divine.
        My Baby!

Two wee dimpled cheeks,
    Velvety soft
Under those little eyes,
    Gazing aloft.
        My Baby!

Elf-like golden hair,
    Crowning the head
That lies on the pillow
    Of tiny bed.
        My Baby!

Smiling when waking,
    Resting awhile,
Smiling when slumbering—
    Always a smile.
        My Baby!

God bless you, baby,
    God send you health
God send you happiness,
    Better than wealth.
        My Baby!

God, keep you darling
    (He alone can),
To comfort your parents,
    When you are a man.
        My Baby![1]

---

1   Written 12th July 1896 and published in *The Manxman*, 17th October 1896, p.4. The poem
reveals Quilliam's sentimentality and idealization of womanhood.

WAITING

O True-Believers, be patient, and strive to excel in patience, and be constant-minded, and fear God, that ye may be happy. Ayat 200 of Sura 3, The Family of Imran, Koran.

Whoso doeth evil shall be rewarded for it; and shall not find any patron or helper other than God; whoso doeth good work, whether such a one be male or female, and is a True-Believer, that one shall be admitted into Paradise, and shall not in the least be unjustly dealt with. Sura 4, Women, Koran.[1]

Work as ye will, God will behold thy work. Sura 9, Koran.[2]

I can wait until the harvest,
    I can wait until the dawn;
I have sown, and with the reaper
    I can wait to claim my own.

I can wait, and still be sowing,
    In due season I shall reap;
If I neither fail nor falter,
    God His promises will keep.

I can wait, for I am resting,
    In perfect promise true,
Made by Him who is Eternal,
    Each shall yet receive his due.

Be it soon, or be it later,
    Harvest will sure come in time;
Come like showers of rain descending
    In the thirsty summer time.

---

1   Sale, 4:124–5, p.90.
2   Sale, 9:105 (partial), p.194.

Why then should the arms grow weary,
    Why the heart despairing cry?
Though the clouds look dark and dreary,
    Yet the sun is in the sky.

Darkness lasts but for a season,
    'Tis dispelled by morning ray;
After winter, summer season,
    After death, Eternal Day.[3]

---

3   Written 1st January 1897 and published in *TC*, Vol.IX, No.209, 13th January 1897, p.26.

THE KEY TO HAPPINESS

The man who is not kind to others need not expect God to be kind to him.
Saying of the Prophet Muhammad.

Sweet is the light of a friendly face;
    Pleasant the ripples of guileless glee;
Why should we miss e'en a glance of grace,
    One to the other, where'er we be?
    Why should we draw from a bitter spring,
    Words that we speak, or songs that we sing?

Trouble and sorrow are always near;
    Failure and conflict make life look dark;
True—but the sigh of a friend sincere
    Soundeth as sweet as the song of the lark.
    Solace for sorrow, or smile to smile;
    Love maketh harmony all the while!

Think then for others, 'tis always best;
    Sweeten the cup that we all must drink;
Bite out your tongue ere you launch the jest;
    Cruel as murder to hearts that shrink:
    Cut off your hand ere you deal a blow,
    Cowardly base, on a fallen foe.

Let not a flicker of wanton play
    Steal from the glow of the hearth at home;
Think not it weak to be drawn away,
    Led by a child when she murmurs, Come!
    Man! Be assured when the loves God-given
    Pluck at your sleeve—you are watched by heaven.

Treasure the heart that of old you won,
  Goodlier treasure than hoards of gold;
If you lose Love, you are all undone!
  Deadliest death is a life grown cold!
  Love is the key to the heavenly door;
  Man! will you lose it for evermore?[1]

---

1 *TC*, Vol.IX, No.219, 24th March 1897, p.183.

THE TRUE EASTER

The pious who believe in the mysteries of faith, who observe the appointed times of prayer, and distribute alms out of what We have bestowed on them, and who believe in that revelation which hath been sent down onto thee (O Mohamad!), and that which hath been sent down to the prophets before thee, and have a firm assurance in the life to come: these are directed by their Lord, and they shall prosper. Sura 2, Verses 2–5, Koran.

Be constant in prayer, and give alms, and what good ye have been sent before for your souls, ye shall find it with God; surely Allah seeth that which ye do. Sura 2, Verse 110, Koran.

When a man dies, his fellow-creatures ask, How much wealth has he left behind him; but the angels inquire, How many good deeds has he sent before him. Traditional saying of the Prophet Mohamed.

From one's mere self, to rise above
    All hate and lust and pride,
To soar aloft, like winged dove,
    With faith, whate'er betide.

This is the resurrection time—
    Not Easter morn alone,
But every day striving anew
    More perfect to have grown.

This shall the soul find perfect peace—
    Al Jannat! Blessed abode!
Where cares and troubles all do cease,
    Lost is the weary load.

So may all Muslims rise each day,
    In goodness, truth, and love;
From worldly troubles pass away
    To lasting bliss above.

And when their eyes are clos'd in death,
    And men count worldly store,
May angels chant, with fragrant breath,
    Their good deeds sent before.[1]

---

1   Written 12th April 1897 and published in *TC*, Vol.IX, No.222, 14th April 1897, p.229.

A JANAAZA ODE
TO THE MUSLIM WARRIORS WHO FELL IN THE GRECO-TURKISH WAR[1]

Gather the sacred dust
    Of warriors true and bold,
Who bore the flag of a nation's trust,
Who fell in a cause victorious, just,
    And died like heroes of old.

Gather them one and all—
    From Redif to Beyler Bey;[2]
Come they from cottage or palace hall,
They fell for Islam, for them shall fall
    The tears of Muslims always.

Gather the corpses strewn
    O'er many a battle plain;
From many a grave that lies so lone,
Without a name, aye without a stone—
    Gather the noble slain.

We care not whence they came—
    For dear is their lifeless clay—
Whether unknown, or known to fame,
Their cause and faith were all the same,
    They died—Muslims all were they.

Where'er the brave have died—
    Though their dust may sleep apart,
Living they struggled side by side;
And e'en grim death cannot divide
    The Muslim true heart from heart.

---

1   Another of Quilliam's poems that refers to historical events. In this case the Turkish–Greek Wars fought between the Ottoman Empire and Greece in 1897. Its immediate cause was over the status of the Ottoman province of Crete. An ode is an elaborately structured poem in praise of a hero or a famous event. Quilliam uses "ode" in the classical sense and commemorates the fallen Ottoman troops as heroes. The Arabic "janaaza" refers to a funeral.
2   Redif, the reserve force in the Ottoman army; Beyler Bey, a commander-in-chief.

Gather their sacred clay,
    Wheresoe'er it may rest—
Where they fought in the bloody fray,
Where they fell on the battle day,
    Be it East or be it West.

The Giaour[3] may not dread
    This gathering of the brave,
They march but with a soundless tread,
'Tis the shades of the deathless dead
    Who come from each noble grave.

Your tears they do not crave,
    Their souls in Paradise rest,
Their dull, cold bodies may sleep in the grave,
But never will fade the fame of the brave
    Who fought for the truth with zest.

They live, they are not dead;
    'Tis only the living weep;
The men who were by Edhem[4] led,
And the hearts that together bled,
    Together now can calmly sleep.[5]

---

3   "Giaour" (Turkish: Gâvur) is an offensive Turkish word for infidel or non-believer and is similar to the Arabic word "kafir". The term was used in English literary circles: Lord Byron's poem "The Giaour" was published in 1813.
4   Edhem Pasha, a Turkish Field Marshall, who had overall command of the Ottoman forces.
5   Written 24th May 1897 and published in *TC*, Vol.IX, No.228, 26th May 1897, p.327.

THE MUSLIM'S EVENING PRAYER

O Thou who gavest life, who causeth death,
Watch o'er me now I lay me down to sleep;
My body rest, renew, as Thou hast saith
Thou wilt for those that Thy commandments keep!
Let no thought of the morrow cause my pain,
Nor fearsome dreams disturb nocturnal rest;
So health and vigour renew'd I may gain
To work for Thee as Thou may deem it best;
If it be for me that earth no more shall be,
And that the thread of life for me has run,
I bow my head to Thy Divine decree,
And trust my deeds Thy fav'ring glance have won.
Whate'er betides, in peace I lay me down to rest,
Resign'd to fate, because, Allah, Thou knowest best.[1]

---

1   Another poem on the topic of the Evening Prayer, written at Peel, Quilliam's hometown on
     the Isle of Man, 26th September 1897, and published in *TC*, Vol.X, No.244, 6th October 1897,
     p.631.

A CHEER FOR THE MEN WHO LOSE!

Here's to the men who lose!
E'en though their work be e'er so nobly plann'd
    And watched with zealous care,
No glorious crown rewards their efforts grand;
    Contempt is failure's share.

Here's to the men that lose!
When loud cheers and bright smiles our efforts greet
    The work is easy then;
The Hero, he, who after dire defeat,
    Stands up and fights again.

Here's to the men that lose!
The ready plaudits of the fawning crowd
    Salute the victor's ears;
Not a grain of sympathy is allowed
    To him who needs the cheers.

Here's to the men that lose!
'Tis to the non-successful that I sing,
    Whose merits you refuse;
A well-thought failure is a noble thing;
    Here's to the men that lose![1]

---

1   Written 10th October 1897 and published in *TC*, Vol.XI, No.265, 9th February 1898, p.92, and probably an expression of Quilliam's own feelings at the time about his efforts to establish Islam in the UK. An early example of an anti-hero sentiment.

OH DEATH! WHERE IS THY STING?

Why should one fear the approach of death?
Is it not mere cessation of breath?
Is this life all we live for? Isn't the end
Of all our hopes to which our footsteps tend?
If so, then drink and bid dull sorrow fly;
Let's merry be, for tomorrow we must die.
Virtue is folly, pleasure is the game;
Why should we care? In death we're all the same.
A fig for wisdom! 'tis but a foolish name:
An empty bubble that which men call fame.
Today is ours, tomorrow—who can tell!
The bells may chime! Well let them ring a knell.
'Tis all the same: Death ends it all, you know;
We'll sow the wind, the reaping may be slow.
The reaping did we say? Ah, there's the sting!
To our minds this doth the question bring
That needs must have an answer. O this Death!
'Tis not thee that's fear'd; What's done, what's saith,
In life 'tis that which is the cause of fear,
Gives anguish to the mind, the eye a tear.
But if the actions of the past are just,
They'll soar aloft and leave the earthy dust,
From earth it came; it doth return to earth:
The spirit loos'd enjoys a second birth,
And opens its eyes on a fairer scene,
An ever cloudless day. 'Tis so I ween.
And if 'tis so, and gone forever care,
The face of death is not black but fair.
Thou cometh, Death, thou cometh as a friend!
I wait for thee; God knoweth when to send.[1]

---

1   Quilliam returns to a common theme, death, mortality and the Afterlife. Written 11th February
     1898 and published in *TC*, Vol.XI, No.266, 16th February 1898, p.108; reprinted in *The
     Manxman*, 26th February 1898, p.17.

MARCH

The March winds are blowing and sighing,
    And bursting with many a roar;
As if it 'twas a great giant dying,
    And struggling as in days of yore.
They fright us as we rest on the pillow,
    And compel us to think of the sea,
And of those who are tossed on the billow
    By this March wind so wild and so free.
We see the waves flashing and crashing,
    And foaming across the broad strand,
While wild horses break and are dashing
    'Gainst the rocks of our own native land
The trump of the March wind is blowing
    Like steeds that one hears from afar,
And louder and fiercer 'tis growing—
    The last blasts of wintery war
And yet we joy in the midst of our quaking,
    For we know, with its shrieks and its yell,
The grim chains of the frost king are breaking,
    And the earth will be clear of its spell.
And March, roaring March, is now dying,
    Its requiem gladly we'll sing,
Its soughing and blowing and sighing
    But herald the coming of Spring.[1]

---

1   Written 24th March 1898 and published in *TC*, Vol.XI, No.272, 30th March 1898, p.203.

WORK AND WAIT AND WORK AGAIN

Have you ever, in the garden,
    Noticed life in low estate?
Seen the worm, the caterpillar,
    Crude of form and slow of gait?
Have you noticed, when obstructed,
    That the worm has learn'd to wait?

Out of ashes rose the Phoenix.
    Through our trials shines success
But unless we make the effort
    A life struggle, and no less,
Can we hope the victor's laurels
    Will our sweated brows caress.

So when check'd in further effort
    Or when we do failure meet,
We must not turn back dishearten'd,
    But, with worm-like patience, greet
Time, who swallows every failure,
    And who leaves all things complete.

Never let your footsteps waver,
    Keep your line of action straight,
Don't forget the caterpillar,
    And in patience learn to wait;
Then success will crown your efforts,
    Perfect peace your final fate.[1]

---

1   *TC*, Vol.XI, No.284, 22nd June 1898, p.396.

THE ANGEL MESSAGE

Teach me, O Allah! Thou whom we adore;
Instruct me now from out Thy wisdom's store,
The reason why Thou, being just and good,
Permitteth evils to exist, which could
By e'en one word from Thee dispelled be.
Successful fraud, disease, and misery—
These reign enthroned, while virtue stands reluctant
And watches vice oppose it with impunity;
Is this Thy justice? This Thy constant zeal
To all that tendest to the common weal?
To strengthen those who all Thy laws oppose,
Permit the weak to be crushed by their foes;
Why should'st Thou thus, over all around,
Leave vice to triumph and virtue confound?
O Allah! Speak! The reason to me state.
I heard a sound, it came from Heaven's gate,
And I looked up and saw an angel there;
It came and brought an answer to my prayer—
And smiling spoke the white one from above:
"Is earth a spot for heav'n-born souls to love?"[1]

---

1   Written 20th July 1898 and published in *TC*, Vol.XII, No.289, 27th July 1898, p.42.

COOILL IN GILL[1]

Ye laughing streamlet
    With your merry song
'Midst flow'ry banks set
    As ye dash along,
I stand by your brink
    And list to your lay
And hard strive to think
    What your murmurings say,
And methinks as I listen
    And puzzle my brain,
I admire how you glisten
    And catch the refrain:

"High up upon the mountain,
    Yet not far from this spot,
Gushes a little fountain
    From 'neath a ferny grot.[2]
'Tis from there I come flowing,
    A streamlet pure and clear,
And onward I am going
    Light-hearted, free from fear,

Here gushing and there pushing
    Impatient long to stay,
And forward ever rushing
    Anxious to get away.
As I sing, I go dashing
    Across green field and vale,
O'er pebbles I go splashing
    Like a ship in full sail.

---

1   Quilliam explains that the estate of Cooill-in-Gill is in the parish of Marown, Isle of Man. The
    river in the poem runs through the estate, finally losing itself in the River Dhoo. He notes that
    throughout the eighteenth century the estate was occupied by persons of the name "Quilliam"
    and speculates that Cooill-in-Gill was originally "Quilliam's Gill".
2   Grotto.

Over rocks how I tumble
  And fast scurry along,
Through a gorge now I rumble
  With slow murmuring song,
Through an old-fashioned garden
  I so peacefully glide,
I am sure I ask pardon
  To intrude on its pride:

But I ne'er cease my running
  And swift pass through the glade,
For I get there no sunning
  For the trees cast their shade.
The gath'ring my forces
  With heart not afraid,
I seek for new courses
  And leap the cascade.

For a moment I stay
  Within a dark pool,
Then I'm off and away
  From shelter so cool.
My song now I'm changing
  From roar to a coo,
And tired of free-ranging,
  I am lost in the Dhoo."

Ah streamlet, I've listed
  To your rippling sweet song,
To learn which, I'd wisted[3]
  As you rush'd there along.
'Tis a story you telling
  Not of streamlet alone,
But of all that are dwelling
  Within the world's zone.

---

3   Wist, i.e. "become aware", archaic variant of "wit".

'Tis from sources as humble
 That at first we arise,
That onward so we tumble—
 Hasty, heedless, unwise.
In our youth forward rushing,
 Ever scorning to wait,
Helter-skelter and pushing,
 Till we learn when too late,

That our rush was a mad one,
 That we've wasted our breath,
That our end is a sad one—
 The black waters of death.[4]

4 Written 18th November 1898 and published in *TC*, Vol.XII, No.306, 23rd November 1898, pp.316–17.

ODE TO THE MEMORY OF
GENERAL GHAZI HAFIZ PASHA

Who died on the 19th April, 1897, a martyr's death, fighting for the holy religion of Islam against the Giaours (Greco–Turkish War).

Unroll his turban! Lay his sword aside!
His fight is ended—bid the cannons cease;
'Twas Islam's banner under which he died,
For him has God proclaimed eternal peace!
Cover'd with scars, the fallen hero lies,
No more to hearken to the loud alarms
Of cannon booming and the battle-cries—
"*Allah Akbar*"! Islam! Muslims to arms!

In gruesome heaps, the dying and the dead,
The Muslim and the Christian, there are laid
On the Thessalian plain, where their tread
On the green verdure soft impressions made.
And Hafiz Pasha lies there 'mongst the slain,
Who on the morn was full of manly pride,
Maimed and disfigured, true! but freed from pain—
Allah reward! For Islam 'twas he died.[1]

---

1   Another memorial poem written in praise of a fallen Ottoman military commander who has
     lost his life in the Greco–Turkish conflict. Quilliam explains the context in the poem's sub-
     title. General Ghazi Hafiz Pasha was killed at the age of 82 at the Battle of Malounas Pass. He
     reportedly was advancing at the head of his troops on horseback when wounded twice (arm and
     hand) but he refused to dismount or give up command. He then received a fatal shot through
     the mouth and spinal cord. Brent Singleton (ed.), *The Convert's Passion: An Anthology of Islamic
     Poetry from the Late Victorian and Edwardian Britain.*(USA: Borgo Press, 2009), p.131. Published
     in *TC*, Vol.XIII, No.334, 7th June 1899, p.363.

A VISION OF PARADISE

One eve as I sat at the casement
    And gazed out at the western sky,
I beheld there such wondrous splendor
    I felt as if heaven were nigh:
It appeared as if angel fingers
    Had thrown open the portals wide,
And given a glimpse of the glory
    Of the shore on the other side.

I thought as I gazed on the picture—
    The fairest that ever I'd seen—
I could see the high hills of glory
    And the lovely valleys between;
It seemed as if mounted on Borak,[1]
    Like the Prophet of Allah I rode
And soar'd thro' the seven heavens,
    And saw where the angels abode.

I heard the sweet plashing of fountains
    As they fell in silvery spray;
I heard the sweet chanting of song-birds
    Carolling their heavenly lay;
I saw the immense verdant branches
    Of the Lote tree[2] spread far and wide;
In their shade bask'd heavenly houris,
    While flowers grew on every side.

---

1   *Al-Buraq*, the winged steed that Muhammad rode on between Mecca and Jerusalem before ascending through the seven heavens to meet his Lord.
2   The Lote Tree is described in the Qur'an as "shrouded in mystery unspeakable". Muhammad was accompanied by the Angel Jibril (Gabriel) to this point during the Ascension (*Mi'raj*). The tree has been interpreted in myriad ways by commentators, but all agree that it marks an utmost boundary after which there is only the mystery of God.

I saw there a great throne all golden:
　　　　It shone with so brilliant a glare
That mine eyes grew glazed with beholding,
　　　　So I faintly muttered a prayer.
I saw near that great throne of glory
　　　　A form noble, tender and rare,
And my heart gave a throb of rapture,
　　　　For I knew the Prophet was there.

It was not merely a fancy,
　　　　This sweet sunset vision of mine,
The portals of heaven are ever
　　　　Flung open at evening time,
That those then whose time is appointed
　　　　May cast on one side earthly ills,
And soar to the heavenly regions
　　　　And walk by those bright sparkling rills.

When for me then life's sunset cometh,
　　　　And my mortal wanderings cease,
And when I do pass through those portals
　　　　To enjoy the eternal peace,
I am sure that I shall remember
　　　　In those regions so fair and far
My so strange yet beautiful vision
　　　　Of those bright sunset gates ajar.

Maybe while I sat there so gazing
　　　　At that vision of regions blest,
The freed soul of some True-Believer
　　　　Entered into eternal rest,
Pass'd thro' those bright sunshiny portals
　　　　Joying at his recent release,
And shouting with rapturous pleasure,
　　　　Found sweet rest and eternal peace.

Pressing forward joying and joyous,
  Happy to receive his reward,
Well pleased that his labours did merit
  Approval from Allah, the Lord.
May such be all yours, be my portion
  When on earth our labours are o'er;
May we also wing our flight yonder,
  And dwell on that heavenly shore.[3]

---

3 Written 28th July 1899 and published in *TC*, Vol.XIV, No.343, 9th August 1899, p.91.

TO A BLUE-BELL GROWING IN A MANX LANE

Hail, little blue-bell! bell of blue,
    Growing on the roadside bank,
Wee fairy bell of tender hue
    Smiling mids't the weeds so rank.

How I love to see you growing,
    Looking like a turquoise gem;
Emerald leaves around you showing—
    Setting for a diadem.

With your head bending so lowly,
    Like a blushing little maid,
Emblem thou of meekness holy,
    Innocence and manners staid.

Now a lesson come and teach us,
    Little flow'r in humble place;
Let its tender message reach us
    With a sweet poetic grace.

Though our place be low and humble,
    We can make our lives sublime,
If we work and do not grumble,
    Fill our little niche of time.

And when wintry blasts, so chilling,
    Cause the flow'r to lose its hue,
From its calyx find distilling
    Some clear drops of honey dew.[1]

---

1   Written at Quilliam's family home at Onchan, Isle of Man, 13th August 1899 and published in
    TC, Vol.XIV, No.344, 16th August 1899, p.106; *The Manxman*, 16th September 1899, p.10.

ISLAMIC RESIGNATION I

Thou only Allah giv'st me light
'Tis Thee who makes the future bright,
Dispel the gloom of doubt away
And heareth when to Thee I pray.

Though sore the trials of the day,
Thou hast decreed, so I obey,
And murm'ring not at Thy decree
Allah, my all I yield to Thee.

I know this weary, anxious breast
With Thee will find eternal rest;
And knowing this, I do resign
My will, O Allah! Unto Thine.

My earthly friends though few they be,
And chill the looks that fall on me,
I rest content, full well I know,
Who trusts in Thee need fear no foe.

I work, I wait, while here I live
For the reward 'tis Thine to give,
Content to leave my future fate
With Thee, Allah, Compassionate![1]

---

1   Written 22nd August, 1899 and published in *TC*, Vol.XIV, No.345, 23rd August 1899, p.123.

THE SONG OF THE MANX FISHER GIRL

As softly blows the cool breeze
    From off the sea,
I feel that is wafting
    My love to me,
Whilst there up in the heavens afar,
I see a bright and glowing star
That seems to speak and tell this tale,
He cometh home to Nancy Quayle,
    Doth John Cregeen.

So kindly blows the cool breeze
    From off the sea,
I am sure it bringeth quickly
    My John to me;
I hear it murmur in the breeze,
I hear it rustling in the trees;
Its voice is clear; it tells this tale,
He cometh home to Nancy Quayle,
    Doth John Cregeen.

The wind blows cool this morning
    From off the sea;
But still, alas, my loved one
    Is far from me.
Oh, woe is me! I moan and sigh;
Oh! Why did I e'er heed their tale
He cometh not to Nancy Quayle,
    Doth John Cregeen.

The wind blows fresh this evening
  From off the sea;
I hope it means not danger
  To John ma chree.
Why, there's his boat, I know the sail,
I knew right well he would not fail.
The wind spoke true, blow soft, blow gale.
He cometh home to Nancy Quayle
  Dear John Cregeen.[1]

---

1 A Manx folk poem written 26nd August 1899 and published in *TC*, Vol.XIV, No.346, 30th
  August 1899, p.138; *The Manxman*, 30th September 1899, p.10.

TO MY SON, R. AHMED QUILLIAM BEY, ON THE 19TH ANNIVERSARY OF HIS BIRTHDAY

My son, another year has fled away,
    And scarce a cloud obscur'd the azure sky
Of infancy and youth, scarcely a day
    But joy hath strewn bright flowers to greet thine eye.

For thou hast had thy parents' watchful love
    And patient guardianship and tender care;
My son, no love in after years can prove
    So pure and true as such as children share.

The world to thee is yet unknown, and thou
    Like all young men, art full of hope and joy;
May e'er thy future be as bright as now
    With happiness which time can never cloy.

I do not pray that thou throughout thy life
    May never know the weight of care and grief;
Each man that passes through the world's hard strife
    From troubles ne'er can find complete relief.

And well it is so. Thus our eyes can see,
    The vanities of earth, and thus discern
The path of happiness and peace, and we
    To pure and all-enduring joys may turn.

Trust not the world; its acts deceitful are,
    And seek not all its pleasures to explore;
A canker worm does worldly pleasures mar,
    True happiness it hath not in its store.

These thoughts, mayhap, you think are sad to breathe
    To you upon what is your natal day,
When all your friends their festive garlands wreathe
    Their wishes for you—all that's bright and gay.

But I well know that grief can reach the heart
    E'en when the sun of youth shines bright and clear;
A cloud may come, and all our smiles depart,
    And we are robbed of all we hold most dear.

It may hap so to thee, but earnestly
    I pray Allah to save thee from such woe,
And cause all comforts to be showered on thee,
    With all the joys that true affections show.

Thy lot on earth, I pray may be
    Bless'd with contentment, calm with peace and health;
And friends trusted and tried I wish for thee—
    Better by far than luxury and wealth.

That o'er life's sea that thou may'st sail in peace,
    Thy actions such that none can cause thee fie;
That when at last thy soul shall find release,
    In certain hope and trust then thou'st may die.

Secure in knowing, though thy life be o'er,
    So far as this world and its cares betide,
That sin and grief are gone for evermore,
    And peace and joy eternally abide.[1]

---

1   One of several poems in which we glimpse Quilliam's feelings towards a family member, in this
     case, his oldest son, Robert Ahmed Quilliam (1879–1954). Written 1st September 1899 and
     published in TC, Vol.XIV, No.347, 6th September 1899, p.155.

THE HUMAN PARADOX

There was a man, an oddish man,
 Who lived some time ago;
The neighbours said that he was fast,
 And yet his name was "Sloe".

He had a dog, a little dog,
 He found it in the park
He called that dog "Chinchona", for
 He knew it by its bark.

Now Sloe he loved a maiden fair:
 She was a tasteful doll
Her surname it was Parrot, but
 Her Christian name was Poll.

Now Sloe he was a jokey chap,
 With observations queer,
He said he ne'er would fill a grave,
 Yet oft was full of beer.

One Monday he a-fishing went
 But caught no trout nor dab,
But when he took to rowing,
 Then he found he'd caught a crab.

When Sloe got tired of single bliss
 He tried the other plan,
And lo! Behold, he found a wife
 There in the Isle of Man!

He never used to watch the time,
 So swiftly did it glide;
His watch a Waterbury was,
 With running spring inside.

When after twenty years had passed,
    His wife was first to go,
Says he, they cannot bury me,
    Although I am a Sloe!

And now I'm free, I'll go to see
    The countries of the earth.
He went; but saw no foreign lands,
    For he died in his berth.[1]

---

1   One of Quilliam's humorous folklore poems through which he always provides an inner
    understanding of the human condition, in this case the inevitability of death. Written 2nd
    October 1899 and published in *TC*, Vol.XIV, No.351, 4th October 1899, p.215; *The Manxman*,
    4th November 1899, p.10.

THE DEATH OF ABDULLAHI

Fierce the battle raged,
A hail of bullets, from the murderous Maxim gun,
Fell all around, and swept the field.
                    Brave sons of Islam,
From the burning suns of the Soudan
Rushed forward, fighting for
Their fatherland and faith,
Only to meet a bloody death,
And earn a martyr's crown.
In the thickest of the fray,
Where danger was the greatest,
And the fiery hail fell fastest,
Rode Abdullahi-bin-Sayid Mohammad
Whom men had called the Khalifa.
At his right hand his bold lieutenant,
Ahmed Fedil, rode;
And many a gallant emir
Swelled the martial train.
If human bravery ere deserved
A victory to gain, that day should
Victor's laurels rest upon the brow
Of the untameable son of the Soudan;
But Allah willed it not.
Under the pitiless iron hail
Son after son of the desert sank,
Never to rise again.
But fifty-three gallant warriors,
The flower of Muslim chivalry,
The bravest of the very brave,
At last were left to contend
'Gainst iron guns which vomited death
And hellish smelling flames and smoke,
Further resistance 'twas in vain.
"Now yield ye, Abdullahi!"

Came the cry from the invading force.
"I yield to God alone", replied the warrior chief;
Then turned he unto the dark-skinned Youssuf
And said, "Bring hither unto me
The white sheep-skin on which
My predecessor sat". 'Twas brought,
And straightaway from his Arab steed
Abdullahi leapt, and in a voice of stern command
Addressed his warriors thus—
             "Oh noble Emirs!
'Tis great Allah's will we die,
Then let us meet our death as Muslims."
So saying he sat down the sheepskin rug upon,
And gathered around him sat his bodyguard.
             Again the cannon roared,
And belched forth its tongue of flame.
Down, down they all sank to the ground;
Death had claimed them for its own;
Abdullahi shot through head, heart, arm and leg,
And all faithful emirs perished.
It was thus that Abdullahi died.[1]

---

1   Quilliam's note states that Abdullahi-bin-Sayid Mohammad had been the khalifa to the Mahdi
    of Soudan and had succeeded him to the leadership after the Mahdi's death at the Battle of
    Omdurman. Abdullahi's forces had been defeated by the British on 24th November 1899.
    Written on 10th December 1899 and published in *TC*, Vol.XIV, No.361, 13th December 1899,
    p.371.

THE LAST JOURNEY

When the clouds are dark and dreary
        At the close of mortal way;
When with falt'ring footsteps weary
        I am going home to stay—
        Evermore to stay.

Then I think of lov'd ones parted
        From me now full many a day,
And I feel quite blythe-hearted,
        I am going home to stay—
        Evermore to stay.

Absence makes the heart grow fonder,
        At least so the poets say;
And there'll be no parting yonder
        I am going home to stay—
        Evermore to stay.

Though alone the path I travel
        Though my mortal powers decay,
My feet tread upon sure gravel
        I am going home to stay—
        Evermore to stay.

Be it late, or be it early,
        Comes the call I must obey;
Cheerfully I'll meet it, fairly
        I am going home to stay—
        Evermore to stay.[1]

---

1   In December 1899, two pioneer converts, Elizabeth Leylah Warren and John Ali Hamilton, died. Their deaths affected Quilliam deeply and the poem was composed with their deaths on his mind. Written 17ᵗʰ December 1899 and published in *TC*, Vol.XIV, No.362, 20ᵗʰ December 1899, p.394.

THE SAD LAY OF THE MUSICAL MAN

There was a man with a musical taste
    Though a *crotchet* his friends said he had got;
He tried to write in a musical way,
    And *quavered* so much that he made a blot.

"That's somewhat bad with a *piano* tone",
    He inwardly mutter'd, "I'll make no more";
But he soon found to be musical still,
    It was *comme il faut* he should make a score.

He was born, 'twas said, in the month of *March*;
    And his origin was *so low*, they said,
That his parents their clothes often did place
    In a shop with a *trio* of balls o'erhead.

He was sent to school, and he went with *glee;*
    There were *forty* boys in the class as well.
He learnt his lessons, and when he got top
    He thought, "*In Deed* I'm no end of a *swell*".

And still pursuing his musical fad,
    He left his house and lived in a *flat;*
In *Arpeggio* Square, by a streak of luck,
    He found a place that suited him pat.

His shrill voice, he said, was a *mild alto,*
    Though his neighbours said that was not the case,
For they'd wager a *tenner*, in *treble* quick time
    That his voice and actions were terribly *base.*

One morning he took a very bad cold,
    And wrote to his doctor a *note* in rhyme,
And *E* said *B sharp* and come to *A flat*
    And do please to *C* me in *quickstep* time.

The doctor came and examined him close,
   And said, "I'll send you a little dram,
Of which you must take just a *minim* dose,
   And a pill or two down your throttle cram.

The physic came, and the physic he took,
   But his *organs* it didn't affect at all
And in twenty-hours his *pipes* were stopp'd—
   They play'd o'er his corpse, "The Dead March in Saul".

During his life he sang many a *chant*
   And many a *tune* he did often *play*;
And his ruling passion was strong in death
   And there in the grave *so low* he did *lay*.[1]

---

1   A comedic play on words that shows the Sheikh's playful side but, on a more serious note,
    portrays mortality; *TC*, Vol.XV, No.374, 14th March 1900, p.154.

WHEN DOES A WOMAN TRULY LOVE?

When is it that the woman learns true love,
    Which in her heart eternal springs;
When it o'er her—she a babe—
    Sweet lullabies her mother sings?

No; that is not the time her heart awakes,
    And feels aglow true love's hot fire;
The babe just coos in unison;
    What more can mother's heart desire?

Is it when with virginal blushes deep,
    She modestly hung down her head,
As in her ear a gallant youth
    His tale of amorous passion said?

No; that is not the time, though she thinks so,
    And fondly pictures in her mind
A world of happiness and bliss
    With him who seems so good, so kind.

But time, alas! another tale does tell,
    And when, too late, maybe is found
A lover's word is light as air,
    And, like the air, cannot be bound.

Is it when marriage vows are made—
    A covenant to last for life;
And trusting to a plighted troth,
    The maid is merged into wife?

No, it is not then; for often the dream
    Of eternal marital bliss
Vanishes when put to the test,
    And proves as transient as a kiss.

When is it, then, the woman learns true love?
    Once more, the question grave I ask;
Nor think ye that it is in sport,
    Your mind to answer I would task.

Is it not when, with mother's joyful heart,
    Her babe she presses to her breast,
With it her heart responsive throbs:
    Nor need for love again to quest?

From out her heart a fountain gushing wells
    Of love so pure, so good, so true,
That out of Paradise itself
    Must come the plant from which it grew.[1]

1   Written in Budapest, Hungary, April 7th, 1900, and published in *TC*, Vol.XV, No.383, 16th May
     1900, p.315.

NIGHT THOUGHTS

Have you ever awaked from slumber
    In your bed as you lay at night,
And noticed the stars without number,
    How they shed their silvery light?
The deep stillness you bewildered,
    You felt how vast was the space,
And wondered as you considered
    Of the Power that gave them their place.

Perhaps, as you thus lay gazing
    Up at the star-spangled sky,
To add to your deep amazing
    An aerolite darted by.
Could it be that an angel zealous
    Had seen an intruder near,
And, of heaven's sanctity jealous,
    Had thrown from those regions clear

A flaming dart at the *giaour*,
    Warning him from there to flee,
Demonstrating thus the power
    Of the Mighty One there be
Who placed those lamps so resplendent,
    Who caused to blaze as a sun
Those stars with their light transcendent?
    La Allah ill'allah, the One![1]

---

1   Noting that *ilah* has been replaced by *Allah* in the declaration of faith in the poem's last line; *TC*,
    Vol.XVI, No.392, 18th July 1900, p.41; *IW*, Vol.VI, No.71, 4th August,1901, p.312.

UNTITLED (1900A)

We have passed the noonday summit,
    We have left the noonday heat,
And down the hillside slowly
    Descend our wearied feet.
Yet the evening air is balmy,
    And the evening shadows sweet.

Our summer's latest roses
    Lay withered long ago;
And e'er the flowers of autumn
    Scarce keep their mellowed glow.
Yet a peaceful season woos us,
    Ere the time of storms and snow,

Like the tender twilight weather
    When the toil of day is done;
And we feel the bliss of quiet
    Our constant hearts have won,—
When the vesper planet blushes,
    Kissed by the dying sun.

So falls that tranquil season,
    Dew-like, on soul and sight,
Faith's silvery star-rise blended
    With memory's sunset light,
Wherein life pauses softly
    Along the verge of night.

'Tis so our sister yielded
    The breath of mortal life;
'Tis so she ceased the struggle
    Of this fierce worldly strife;
And saying, "it is over,"
    She winged her spirit flight.[1]

---

1   Untitled, but recited as part of Quilliam's lecture, "Our Departed Friends", described as a tribute
    to two members of the Liverpool Muslim Institute, Thomas Ridpath (1860–1900) and Fatima E.
    Cates (1865–1900), who both passed away on the same day. However, as it stands, the poem is
    clearly a tribute to Fatima Cates: she was an early convert and an important founding member of

A PLEA IN ABATEMENT[1]

I'm foolish, you think, when sometimes you see
    I give to a child a copper or so,
When there in the street barefooted he be,
    And beggeth for alms as past him I go.

Well, perhaps you are right and I am wrong,
    Perhaps I am foolish, tender, and weak;
But, still, I can't help, as I pass along,
    To feel for the poor more than I can speak.

And there's something within that tells to me
    In accents quite plain, so strong and so clear,
That an action well meant wrong cannot be
    If done with intent to comfort and cheer.

What though "those beggars are most of them bad?"
    What though their whining is part of a plan?
Still I'll be foolish and follow my "fad"
    And help and assist them all that I can.[2]

the Institute. It is unclear whether Ridpath ever converted, although he did occasionally attend the Institute with his two young sons. He regularly advertised his stamp collecting business in *The Crescent* between 1895–1900. Written 4th November 1900, see *TC*, Vol.XVI, No.408, 7th November 1900, pp.300–1.

1   A plea in abatement is a legal term that describes a response by the defendant that does not dispute the plaintiff's claim but objects to its form or the time or place where it is used.

2   Dated 10th Ramazan, 1318 (1st January 1901) and published in *Manx Sun*, 26th January 1901, p.14. Clearly charity during Ramadan was on the Sheikh's mind.

ODE TO SCANDAL-MONGERS

Ye folks who are fond now of jangle,
    And gloat over your neighbours' misdeeds
And love reputations to mangle,
    And point out that flowers are "but weeds",

I pray you to pause in your chatter,
    And to seriously think of that place,
Where folks who can scandal and flatter,
    Will be met with a pleasing grimace.

The hell where the fiend in his glories
    Sits staring at stones and at putty,
And listens to slanders and stories,
    And some of them p'raps rather smutty.

For 'tis there, most welcome, you'll enter
    For 'tis appropriate to dwell
In that place, of heat the true centre,
    Those who have made of this earth a hell.[1]

---

1   The Sheikh hits out at his opponents by emphasizing Islam's strong moral stance on slander and
     gossip; written on 3rd March 1901 and published in *TC*, Vol.XVII, No.425, 6th March 1901,
     p.154; *IW*, Vol.VI, No.67, ca. October 1901, p.192.

THE DEATH OF THE OLD YEAR

Wan, feeble, and old,
Through the dismal cold,
    Slowly he tottered by,
As rang from the bell
A funeral knell
To the world to tell,
    His end was drawing nigh.

On our room that night,
With its fire so bright,
    He gazed, then turned aside;
Then with dimming eye,
But without a sigh,
He utter'd goodbye,
    And so the Old Year died.

Yes! such was the end
Of our dear old friend;
    Such the way he did die;
He cheerfully went,
For a life well spent
Brings ever content,
    That no one can deny.

In good earnest strife
He had spent his life.
    His mission to fulfil;
And with conscious pride
Then he calmly died,
When God did decide
    His active pulse to still.

His death was not vain
If from it we gain
    A lesson good and true;
'Tis to do our part
With both head and heart,
That when we depart
    We've nothing left to rue.[1]

---

1   *TC*, Vol.XVII, No.429, 3rd April 1901, p.221; *IW*, Vol.VI. No.66, ca. August 1901, p.139.

A MUSLIM HYMN

O Allah, to us ever dear!
    We seek to guide our souls aright
For us there is no cause for fear
    If we do walk in Islam's light.

Thou doth protect, and Thou doth bless
    And Thou doth consolation send
To those who do their faults confess
    And earnest seek their ways to mend.[1]

---

1   Written 6th April 1901 and published in *TC*, Vol.XVII, No.430, 10th April 1901, p.234; *IW*, Vol.
VI, No.67, ca. October 1901, p.191.

MUSLIM ANTHEM

God bless the Muslim cause:
Bless all who keep Thy laws
    And do the right.
Uphold the Muslim band,
In this and every land;
Give them full strength to stand
    Firm in the fight.

Strengthen and help the weak,
And teach us all to speak,
    Thy truth abound.
May love and liberty,
Truth and sweet purity,
With plenteous charity,
    In us be found.

Hear Thou the orphan's cry,
Assuage the widow's sigh,
    The foolish chide.
Let vice no more abound,
But happiness be found
In every home and round
    The world so wide.[1]

---

1   Dated 1st Muharram 1319 (21st April 1901) and published in *TC*, Vol.XVII, No.432, 24th April 1901, p.265; *IW*, Vol.VI, No.67, ca. October 1901, p.188. Perhaps the most controversial of Quilliam's poems and sung to the tune of the British national anthem.

THE WITNESSES

Yon gleaming stars, which yet each passing cloud
    For e'en a time their glory doth obscure,
Declare a truth eternal, clear and loud,
    And testify the same in language pure,
'Tis God, the One, the True, who madeth us shine;
This God is ours, and man is also Thine.

The ocean bearing on expansive breast
    The merchantmen of countries near and far,
Now toss'd with angry waves, now calm at rest,
    Echoes the answer back unto the star—
'Tis God, the One, the True, who made me roll;
The God, O man, of thy immortal soul.

These are not touched by petty deeds of men,
    They are not blurr'd with his deceiving breath,
They shone and roll'd ere he was born, and then
    Shine on and roll when he is spent in death,
'Tis God, the One, for whom they roll'd and shone;
O man, accept thou then this God alone.[1]

---

1   Written at St. Catherine's, Onchan, Isle of Man on 5th August 1901, and published in *TC*, Vol. XVIII, No.447, 7th August 1901, p.94; *Isle of Man Examiner*, 24th August 1901, p.3.

THE GATEWAY OF THE GRAVE

The grave is deep and silent,
    Its secret is its own;
It veils in sombre silence
    A land to us unknown.

The warbling of the song-birds,
    The sunshine all around,
The busy hum of commerce—
    The grave heeds not their sound.

The widow and the orphan,
    Whose tears fall down like rain,
Stand over it lamenting;
    Their cries are all in vain!

The grave, still cold and silent,
    Within its breast of clay,
Still grimly holds its secret
    Until the judgment day.

Yet from no source so surely
    Doth peace and comfort rise:
Only through its dark pathway
    March we to Paradise.

The weary soul, so anxious,
    With grief and toil opprest,
Finds peace within its portals,
    And sweet, eternal rest.[1]

---

1   Written at St Catherine's, Onchan, Isle of Man, 31ˢᵗ August, 1901 and published in *TC*, Vol. XVIII, No.452, 11ᵗʰ September 1901, p.170.

THE KING'S VISIT TO MANXLAND

Ripple gently water blue,
    Sky preserve and azure hue,
Sun shine forth your brightest ray,
    Minstrels tune your sweetest lay,
For safe within Ramsey Bay,
    Mona's King is here this day.

Snaefell high raise your head,
    Crimson blush you heather red,
Sulby's water ripple gay,
    Cushags show your brightest gold,[1]
Smile Peel's castle walls so old,
    Mona's King is here to-day.

Scion of a noble race,
    With his Queen so fair of face,
Viking's daughter so they say,
    Edward's come our isle to see,
Come to visit you and me,
    Mona's King is here to-day.

When the youngster, now so bold,
    Has become quite grey and old,
He will to his grandchild say,
    How all hearts on Mona's Isle,
Danced with joy all the while,
    Mona's King was here this day.[2]

---

1   Cushag or ragwort, the national flower of the Isle of Man.
2   Written at St.Catherine's, Onchan, Isle of Man, September, 1902 and published in *TC*, Vol.XX, No.508, 8th October 1902, p.234; *The Manx Sun*, 1st November 1902, p.9. The poem celebrates the royal visit of Edward VII and his wife, which took place on the 24th and 25th August 1902.

SOME GOOD ADVICE TO SINGLE MEN

O ye that want caressing,
    When ye are full of care,
When woeful pain oppressing;
    Reduce you to despair,
And you require some cheering
    Upon the round of life,
Why do stand a-fearing.
    The remedy's a wife!

You'll find your woe and sorrow
    Will vanish in a trice,
Then why wait 'til tomorrow
    From wedded bliss so nice.
He lives a lonely stranger,
    A miserable thing,
Who fears there lurks a danger
    Within the wedding ring.

He never hears the praises,
    He never knows true love,
Nor feels the fond embraces
    Like manna from above.
He dies with ne'er a tear
    Sympathetic, then shed o'er him,
And round his lonely bier
    No loving ones deplore him.

So, men, just take this calling
    I speak it not in jest,
Cease now at once your fooling.
    For married life's the best
And if you'd end your trouble,
    And lead an easy life,
From single change to double;
    Take to yourself a wife.[1]

---

1   *TC*, Vol.XX, No.513, 12ᵗʰ November 1902, p.310; *The Manx Sun*, 10ᵗʰ January 1903 (noted in *TC*, Vol.XXI, No.522, p.26). A jocular poetic riposte with a serious underlying message to Yahya Parkinson's "The Song of the Despondent Lover", *TC*, Vol.XX, No.512, 5ᵗʰ November 1902, p.301, where Parkinson laments the loss of an unrequited love. Parkinson's jocular rejoinder to Quilliam's poem, "With Apologies to Sheikh Abdullah Quilliam Bey Effendi, Sheikh-ul-Islam", appeared in *TC*, Vol.XX, No.516, 3ʳᵈ December 1902, p.323.

A CORONACH[1] FOR SIR HECTOR MACDONALD[2]

Now lament ye, Oh Scots, in Highland and Lowland,
    Lament for the loss of one gallant and bold
Mourn ye for a hero, forever in foeland
    Fought like a lion or hero of old.

His voice now is silent, his heart beats no longer;
    No more doth the pibroch[3] ring loudly and shrill;
Our hero—and where was one braver or stronger?
    Now lies on his bier, cold clammy, and still.

He stooped not for favour; to none went he cringing;
    By deeds he carved out a niche for his name;
Each field to his brow fresh laurels was bringing,
    Each year adding more to annals of fame.

Daring, perceiving, persevering, achieving,
    The first in the contest the foe to defeat,
On his sword relying, in his judgment believing,
    His men were o'er eager the foemen to meet.

And now he lies silent, on black bier reposing;
    While pibroch wails slowly in notes slow though shrill.
O Hector MacDonald, though your eyes we are closing
    Your name in our hearts is cherished there still.[4]

---

1   A coronach is the traditional improvised singing, usually accompanied by bagpipes, at a death, funeral or wake in the Scottish Highlands. It takes the form of a dirge or keening.

2   Sir Hector MacDonald (1853–1903) was a distinguished Victorian soldier who rose through the ranks and was knighted for his services in the Boer War. The poem may be ironic as it was MacDonald who fought at Omdurman in the Sudan, a victory for British forces that Quilliam had opposed in issuing a *fatwa* and organizing a petition to Parliament. He later committed suicide in Ceylon after a homosexual scandal.

3   Pibroch is a form of music involving elaborate variations on a theme, typically of a martial or funerary character.

4   *TC*, Vol.XXI, No.536, 22nd April 1903, p.251.

ONCHAN HARBOUR

As I watch upon thy shingled shore
    The waves in succession fall,
I catch the sound of a hidden roar
    That echoes with rumbling call.
So the strife of the world and its noise,
    Nor even its fiercest shrieks,
Can not o'erwhelm our griefs and joys
    When the voice of conscience speaks.[1]

---

1   Written at Woodland Towers, Onchan on 7th July 1903 and published in *TC*, Vol.XXII, No.547, 8th July 1903, p.26.

IN MEMORIAM
BRO. JEMAL-UD-DEEN BOKHARI JEFFERY

Yea, now he's gone, the dear old man,
    Our faithful friend is dead;
His manly heart is now at rest
    His soul has heav'nward fled.

He sojourn'd here, through hope and fear,
    For seventy years and three
It will be strange to us
    His face no more to see.

But though we mourn, we do not rave,
    Nor fret, nor yet despond,
For though his body is in the grave,
    His soul has gone beyond.[1]

---

1   Jemal-ud-Deen Bokhari Jeffery (1830–1903) was one of Abdullah Quilliam's oldest friends
    and converted to Islam in 1889. He had played prominent roles within the Liverpool Muslim
    Institute, including Vice-President, and would deputize for the Sheikh when he was away,
    leading the Jumu'a prayers. Written 13th Jomada-as-sani, 1321 and published in *TC*, Vol.XXII,
    No.556, 9th September 1903, p.167.

THE ADVENT OF SPRING

Spring, the enchanter, hath swept o'er the trees,
Wafting his charms on the sweet balmy breeze;
And the boughs yester e'en that were naked and bare
Are now budding anew in the mild, warmer air.

The plants that we thought lay dead on the plain
Have leapt, at his glance, into life once again;
His breath hath dissolved all those glistening gems
Which King Winter had bound on their dark withered stems.

For Summer weaving a bright wreath of flowers,
Old earth refreshing with mild April showers;
From the ground peeps the snowdrop, first flowerlet he brings,
While near the sweet pansy and daffodil springs.

And that sweet aroma which scents all around
Betrays that the primrose has peep'd from the ground;
In gardens more stately on well-cultur'd bed
Shows the dappled crocus its sweet gentle head.

Only one wave of his enchanted wand
Hath such changes made, surprising and grand;
The valleys and meadows are now strewn with flowers;
Methinks he stole them from Elysium's bowers.

And list to the songs that resound in the grove;
The birds e'en are singing a chorus of love.
Then join we in chanting the praises of Spring,
And oft may we greet him and tunefully sing.[1]

---

1   Composed 19th Muharram 1322 (4th April 1904), Woodland Towers, Onchan, Isle of Man; *TC*, Vol.XVIII, No.586, 6th April 1904, p.218; *Reis and Reiyat* (Calcutta), 21st May 1904 (*TC*, Vol. XXIII, No.596, 15th June 1904, p.378).

A B C (ALL BEST COME)

Away Anger
    Always astray,
Let peace descend,
    Abide and stay.

Begone baseness,
    By baseness born,
Let truth instead
    Now sound its horn.

Contentment come,
    Come Cupid coy,
And light the torch
    Of love and joy.

Depart deceit,
    Depart despair,
Sweet peace now come,
    Begone dull care.

Exit envy,
    Erst evil elf,
Love hath no place
    For grasping self.

Foul falsehood fly,
    Fell foulness flee,
No place in heav'n
    Is there for thee.

Go grumbling growls,
    Go greedy gold,
'Tis loving souls
    Who ne'er grow old.

Honour, haste home,
    Honesty hail,
True virtue's power
    Can never fail.

Impertinence,
    Irksome, ill-born,
Ignobly fly,
    Foul, fell, forlorn.

Jealous justice
    Joyfully join
With mercy tender,
    That sterling coin.

Kindliness keep,
    Bickerings cease,
The kindly word
    E'er makes for peace.

Let leasome love
    Lighten labour,
Selfish not be,
    Help your neighbour.

May misery
    Merge into mirth,
Malice depart,
    Slain in its birth.

Needless nonsense
    Never nourish;
Naught that's foolish
    E'er should flourish.

O'er odious
    Ostentation
Open out just
    Indignation.

Peace, perfect peace,
    Peerlessly prize,
Poor pompous pride
    Always despise.

Quarrelsomeness
    Quickly thou quit,
Bear and forebear
    Is maxim fit.

Richest reward
    Rightdoing rends;
Remember God
    The blessing sends.

Selfishness shun,
    Sweet temper shine,
Sly secret sin
    Never be thine.

Temperance true
    Try, taste and test,
'Twill prove to you
    Of friends the best.

Unjust upbraid;
    Unite to heed
Unfortunates,
    Who pity need.

Victorious
    Vanquish vile vice;
Vow villainy
    Thee ne'er entice.

Who wishes weal
    Will wisely walk,
Will work and wait,
    With wise men talk.

eXample show,
　　eXceed, eXcel,
eXpect reward
　　Who doeth well.

Yarely[1] yearn
　　In youthful days,
Your good deeds may
　　Yank yarn of praise.

Zealot not be,
　　Nor zany vain,
With zeal and zest
　　Zenith attain.[2]

1　Eagerly.
2　*TC*, Vol.XXIV, No.604, 10th August 1904, p.92.

DOUGLAS BAY

It's a lovely bay in the dawning, and lovelier still at night,
When the moon shines over Mona's Isle in silvery streams of light;
When the stars appear in the heavens, as they do at the close of day,
And the Howe and Head, like sentinels, both keep watch o'er Douglas Bay.

Behind it, o'er there in the distance, stand the mountains firm and still,
Snaefell, the great giant chieftain, with Barrule and Greba's Hill;
Robed in heather, furze[1] and cushag, while sweet glens all around them lay,
As watch and ward they ever keep over beautiful Douglas Bay.

I've seen it in the summer weather, when the sea basks still in the sun,
When groups of holiday-makers are enjoying their jokes and fun;
Yo ho! they cry for the billows and yo ho! for the oceans play,
There is ever sport and jollity on the shores of Douglas Bay.

I've seen it in grey September when the gales of the equinox roar,
And the waves in tumultuous billows dash in anger 'gainst the shore;
When the sea-bird screams and the wind blows loud thro' all the darksome day,
And with a voice as of thunder roars the sea in Douglas Bay.

Oh it's a bonny bay, my countrymen, at morning, noon and night,
When seen in the bright, fine weather or, when the storm is at its height;
In winter or in summer time, in spring or in autumnal day,
And proud should be each Mona's son of our beautiful Douglas Bay.[2]

---

1   Furze, i.e. gorse.
2   Written at Woodland Towers, Onchan, Isle of Man, 7th September 1904, published in *The Manx Sun*, 24th September 1904, p.8; republished in *The Isle of Man Times*, 17th September 1904, and the *Liverpool Evening Express*, 19th September 1904 (*TC*, Vol.XXIV, No.610, 21st September 1904, p.186).

MY ISLAND HOME

The honeysuckle scents the air,
    And ornaments the hedges,
The gorse and cushag ever fair,
    Gild both the fields and sedges;
The hills are green on ev'ry side,
    With heather on the high land,
Its beauty fills my heart with pride,
    Dear Mona, my own island.

The swallow flying swift and sure,
    In the warm summer weather,
Doth rest awhile on Curragh Mooar[1]
    Amidst the fern and heather;
Its home is in a distant clime
    That's far away from my land,
But well it loves the summer time
    In Mona's little island.

Old England may be rich and great,
    And Erin blythe and jolly,
Stern Scotia grim and so sedate,
    And Gallia melancholy,[2]
But long as fern grows in the glen,
    Or gorse upon the high land,
So long shall you inspire my pen,
    Dear Mona, my own island.[3]

---

1   Manx for great wetlands.
2   Archaic names for Ireland, Scotland and Gaul (France) respectively.
3   Composed 15th September 1904 (7th Rajab 1322), published in *TC*, Vol.XXIV, No.610, 21st
    September 1904, p.186; *The Manx Sun*, 12th November 1904 (*TC*, Vol.XXIV, No.619, 28th
    November 1904, p.330).

MANNIN DY BRAGH![1]

A song for dear Mona, a jubilant song!
    Huzza for the little Manx nation!
So cheer loud-and-long, full-hearted and strong,
    Ye Manxmen of every station,
For land of the glen, of cushag and wren,
    Of mountain, of vale, of heather;
Health to the women, good luck to the men,
    And the island of Mona for ever!

From Douglas, from Ramsey, from wint'ry Peel,
    From Castletown, fill'd with elation,
United we stand, united we feel
    Quite proud of our little Manx nation,
From Aire Point and Garff, to Rushen and Calf,
    United we will all endeavour.
A bumper we'll quaff, a full one, not half,
    Here's the island of Mona for ever!

Three cheers for dear Mona, yes, give them again
    And if anyone seeks information
Why such is your strain, say that your refrain,
    Is cheers for the little Manx nation!
Dear land of the free, sweet isle of the sea,
    Forget you we will not. No, never!
Though years they may flee, our song e'er will be
    Here's the island of Mona for ever![2]

---

1   Isle of Man forever.
2   Written on 8th October 1904 and published in *TC*, Vol.XXIV, No.613, 12th October 1904,
    p.234.

THE RIDDLE OF LIFE

Birth, life and death, three potent words,
    What is it that they spell?
Our entrance in, our life upon,
    Our exit and our knell.

Is that, then, all that is compris'd
    Within those words so said?
And doth the span of passing scene
    Cry "Finish'd" when we're dead?

If such be all, alas for us!
    Poor creatures of an hour,
That bloom unseen, that die forgot,
    Like passing of a shower.

Our days but few, our cares so great,
    And pass'd in toil and strife;
Our life a span, under a ban—
    No blessing, then, is life.

But if the moment of our birth—
    As we believe it be—
Is not just entrance upon earth,
    But immortality;

Then toil and care and meagre fare,
    While on the earth we stand,
Is but precursor, but the path
    That leads to other land.

Then sound of knell doth only tell
    Of life begun for aye—
That perfect life, sans care and strife,
    In the eternal day.[1]

---

1   Written on 16th October 1904 and published in *TC*, Vol.XXIV, No.614, 19th October 1904,
    p.251.

RUSSIA'S "NAVAL VICTORY!"
21ST–22ND OCTOBER

It was the Russian Baltic fleet
    That sail'd in the Northern Sea;
And the skipper that did that fleet control
    Was one Rodjevensky.

He was a bold and gallant tar[1]
    As ever sail'd on the seas;
And he steered away to the Dogger Bank
    In search of Japanese.

He put his spyglass to his eye,
    And scanned both far and near;
"Stand ready!" he cried, "for a foe I've spied:
    Two strange boats do appear."

"They're only small," he loud did call,
    "But so is the dreaded Jap";
Here his hand did shake, and his voice did quake,
    Though he didn't care a rap.

"Get shot and shell," he loud did yell,
    "And your engines at full speed go;
The boats I see it is plain to me
    Are the dreaded torpedo!"

Then came a bang, a sound that rang,
    And echoed far over the sea.
Yet strange it did seem, almost like a dream,
    Not one of the ships did flee.

Twenty minutes passed, "hit one at last!"
    With pride the skipper did cry.
In Russia what glee, o'er this there will be;
    O brave Rodjevensky.

---

1   Tar, a dated informal reference to a sailor.

"We've it one boat, it's scarce afloat,
    Its crew to the bottom will go.
Now quick sail away, and no longer stay;
    I'm a hero, you know.

What reek brave I, for those who die,
    For those my guns have slain?
The blood on my hand is an honour grand,
    And not the least a stain!"

Cowardly skunk, the ship you sunk,
    Away on that Dogger Bank
Was mann'd not by Japs, but by fisher chaps;
    Your deed 'twas murder rank.

The men you slew, there were but two,
    That you killed with a coward's blow;
Fishers though they be, nobler men than ye,
    I'll have you, sir, to know.

For vengeance high, their blood doth cry
    'Gainst thee that did them harm.
And soon, I hope, at the end of a rope
    You'll swing at your yardarm.[2]

---

2   This story was published in the French newspaper, *Le National Illustré*, published in 1904 under the headline banner "Incident Hull Attaque Flotille Pêche Anglaise Rodjevensky Armee Russe". Rodjevensky was an admiral in the Russian navy. *TC*, Vol.XXIV, No.615, 26th October 1904, p.266.

NIL DESPERANDUM![1]

Courage, brother! do not falter,
    Dry your tears and cease from sighing;
Though clouds look black, they soon may alter,
    And the sun will send them flying.

"Out of evil oft cometh good,"
    Is a maxim to my liking;
The blacksmith well the iron beateth,
    But 'tis better for his striking.

Work today and give up grieving,
    Know that joy is born of sorrow;
And though to-day is rainy weather,
    Hap 'twill brighter be to-morrow.

Gambling doth not make our labour
    The least bit more a pleasant task;
'Tis joyful heart that lightens trouble,
    Contentment brings to those who ask.

First the childhood, then the manhood;
    First the task and then the story;
'Tis after nightfall comes the dawning,
    First the shade and then the glory.[2]

---

1   Never despair.
2   Written at Woodland Towers, Onchan, Isle of Man, 23rd October 1904 and published in *TC*,
    Vol.XXIV, No.616, 2nd November 1904, p.282.

THE PERPLEXED BAKER:
THE LAY OF PEMBROKE PLACE

There was a baker blythe and gay,
    And Alfy was his name;
He knew two girls, Pollie and May,
    Both damsels sweet and tame.

Now Alfy liked his cocoa hot,
    And sweet as honeymoon;
When he a cup of cocoa got
    He always had a spoon.

His heart was large, his mind was free,
    But when he went to guzzle,
'Twixt little May and fair Pollie
    His heart got in a puzzle.

They both were nice, they both were smart
    Alas! what could he do?
His mouth was watering for tart,
    Yet he couldn't have the two.

Night after night he eyed the twain,
    But decision could not make
Which one to have; he felt in pain,
    In fact a perfect cake.

Alas! Poor Alf, alack-a-day!
    Each had a pretty face,
Both Pollie prim and handsome May,
    The prides of Pembroke Place.

At last one day said pretty May,
  I'll see what I can do
To make Alf say right straightaway
  Which one he wants of two.

So when he came, with heart aflame,
  His cocoa hot to sup,
She, without shame, the youth to tame,
  Did sweeten well the cup.

This is a treat, this cup so sweet,
  Then Alfy quick did say;
No one can beat you girls so neat,
  Pollie and tricky May.

May, looking blue, said tell me true,
  And tell it out right soon,
Of us girls two which one that you
  Do really want to spoon.

Said Alfy quick, in voice so thick,
  That's more than I can say;
My mind won't stick to make my pick,
  I'll come another day.

Then opening wide the door at side.
  He gently did a slope,
And swift did glide, in fact did slide,
  Like sailor down a rope.

No more his face in Pembroke Place
  Is seen by Poll or May;
Perhaps in space we yet will trace
  The form of Baker A.[1]

---

1 Written in Serres, Turkey-in-Europe, 12ᵗʰ April 1905 and published in *TC*, Vol.XXV, No.640, 19ᵗʰ April 1905, p.254. This poem and the following two are concerned with the morality of choices in romantic love and may suggest a choice that Quilliam is having to make.

A TALE OF THREE MASHERS

This is the story I'm going to state,
 Or rather to give in refrain,
And those who can prate all that I relate,
 Can learn it all over again.

In town there's a boy they call Merry Jim,
 And a girl has he for a flame;
Her headgear so trim, a hat with a brim,
 And Aggie I think is her name.

His pal they call "Col"; his eyes are deep brown,
 Once he did dote upon Eva,
Another maid now he mashes in town,
 Oh Col, are you a deceiver?

A third it is said, they call Fickle Fred,
 And one day with dear little Lu,
Perhaps he will wed, unless and instead
 His promises are not all true.

Such are the crowd, who laugh long and loud,
 As if they were gents of the bar;
They ne'er will be cowed, at least so they've vow'd,
 And sworn by "The Merry White Star."[1]

---

1 *TC*, Vol.XXV, No.643, 10th May 1905, p.295.

TOMMY'S POODLE
A LAY IN DOGGEREL VERSE

Tommy had a little dog,
    Its hair was white as snow,
And everywhere that Tommy went,
    That dog did surely go.

One day it followed Tommy
    On a trip down Rocky Lane,
And very ungallantly
    Did bite the leg of Jane.

"I hope that you are not hurt, Miss,"
    Said Tom, with solemn face;
"If you'll come to the chemist's
    He'll cauterize the place."

Fair Janie took his offer,
    And also took his arm;
Her limping and her anguish
    Quick Tommy's heart did charm.

So when the man of physic
    Had tended to the maid,
Said Tom, "You are too feeble
    To walk home I'm afraid.

"So let me hire a carriage
    And home you thus convey."
Janey said "Thank you much, sir
    But what will your mother say?"

"I'll tell her all about it,
    And I'll take all the blame,
I'll tell her that my stupid dog
    Your pretty leg did maim."

At this the maid consented
    With Tom then home to ride;
He thought it bliss augmented
    To ride thus by her side.

And somehow in the carriage,
    Whilst riding with the Miss,
His thoughts did turn to marriage,
    And he then stole a kiss.

But why prolong the story,
    Or why detain you more,
For Tom and Jane are married,
    And now have kiddies four.

And if their home you visit,
    You'll find residing there
A snappy little puppy
    With beautiful white hair.

And Tom will tell this story
    Of how he met his Jane
Through the snapping by that poodle
    That day in Rocky Lane.

And Jane will smile then sweetly,
    And mildly Tommy rail;
"You silly, foolish fellow
    Why do you tell that tale?"

Then, here's a health to poodle
    And one to Tom and Jane,
May their lives be long and happy
    And ever free from pain.[1]

1   *TC*, Vol.XXV, No.645, 24ᵗʰ May 1905, p.334.

UNTITLED (1905A)

Then labour on: spend and be spent—
    'Tis bliss to do great Allah's will;
It is the path the Prophet went,
    Should not the Muslim tread it still?

Still labour on, though toil thy lot;
    Thy earthly loss is future gain;
Men heed thee, love thee, praise thee not;
    When Allah praises, what is pain?

Go labour on; enough while here,
    If God shall see thee, if He deign
The Muslim's heart to mark and cheer,
    No toil for Islam is in vain.

Go labour on; your hands are weak,
    Your knees are faint, yet do not cease;
Nor falter now, the prize you seek
    Is near—'Tis happiness and peace.[1]

1   Written for the Sheikh's presidential address at the 1905 Annual Meeting of the British Muslim Association and recorded in *TC*, Vol.XXV, No.650, 28th June 1905, p.414.

ISLAMIC RESIGNATION II

I have no wish, oh Allah, but Thy will;
I have no chart but Thy unerring word
Which in the cave the Holy Prophet heard
That blessed night upon bleak Hira's hill.
I trust in Thee, I wait in patience still
For the reward for all that I have wrought,
For good deeds done, for battles grimly fought
'Gainst passion's might and all the hosts of ill.
My inmost heart, my very thoughts are known;
There is no secret hidden, unconfess'd,
For Thou dost search, Oh Allah, every breast,
That power is Thine, and only Thine alone.
So let me live, Oh God, so let my life be passed,
That when I die, I rest with Thee at last.[1]

---

1   Written 10th Shaaban 1323, and published in *TC*, Vol.XXVI, No.665, 11th October 1905, p.230.

ODE TO "THE AUTOCRAT OF ALL THE RUSSIAS"

Tremble now, oh mighty Czar,
"Autocrat" although you are,
Hid in a corner, sound and tight,
In a "devil of a fright."
Tremble now, oh great Czar Nick,
As to power you try to stick;
Rule for you won't last much more,
Czardom's reign is nearly o'er.
List, ye Czar of "Russia's all,"
Hark! The sound of Freedom's call,
Chanting in triumphant staves,
"Perish tyrants! Perish knaves!"
List! The sound now draweth near,
Chant for tyrants grim to fear;
Knell it is of despot's sway,
Harbinger of brighter day.
Day of Freedom, bright and clear,
Day that tyrants well may fear,
The day they fall, undone, unwrung,
Unwept, unhonoured and unsung.[1]

---

1   The Russian Revolution of 1905 was a wave of mass political and social unrest that spread
     through vast areas of the Russian Empire, and was a precursor to the Communist Revolution in
     1917. Quilliam's sympathies are clear. Written 30th Ramazan, 1323 and published in *TC*, Vol.
     XXVI, No.673, 6th December 1905, p.359.

KINDLINESS

Your smiling good-naturedly in your brother's face is charity.
Saying of the Prophet Muhammad.

As fair as the morning,
    And as full of grace,
Is the bright friendly smile
    On a good-natured face.

As firm as a mountain,
    Deny it who can,
Is the grasp of the hand,
    Of the good-hearted man.

As welcome as sunshine,
    True warmth to impart,
Is the sweet kindly word
    From a good-natured heart.

As pure as the dew-drop,
    So tender, so dear,
Is the sympathy shown
    By the good-natured tear.[1]

---

1   Written at Woodland Towers, Onchan, Isle of Man, 6th Ramazan, 1324 (22nd October 1906) and published in *TC*, Vol.XXVIII, No.719, 24th October 1906, p.680.

THE ONWARD PATH

They who fear Allah, and strive to do right
and persevere with patience, upon these
shall no fear come, and they shall attain to
everlasting felicity. Koran[1]

Oh True Believer, let no fear of pain,
Nor friendly favour, nor menace, nor dread,
Divert thee from the path, that thou shouldst tread.
To reach Al-Jannat, where thou wouldst attain;
'Tis not for thee professing Islam's name,
To rest ignoble. Though thy progress slow,
Enough if onward ever it doth show,
So that each daily step advance doth claim,
And helpeth thee to further progress still;
The way to Paradise all onward lies,
Keep Islam's path, nor e'er disheartened be;
And ever yielding to great Allah's will,
Then guidance light and peace will for thee rise,
He loveth those who persevere like thee,
And from all worldly fetters sets them free.[2]

---

1   Verse not identified. It is a loose rendering, probably Quilliam's own, of ideas expressed in 3:200
     and 39:10. It is not based on any English translation published at the time.
2   Written in Liverpool, 12th Ramazan 1324 (28th October 1906) and published in *TC*, Vol.
     XXVIII, No.720, 31st October 1906, p.694.

AFTER MANY YEARS

My own, my sweet, my darling wife,
　　'Tis true that years have made
A change in thee—that 'cross thy brow
　　Some lines old Time hath laid;
And in thy once bright glist'ning hair
　　That cluster'd round thy head,
Some little locks just here and there,
　　Now shine like silv'ry thread;
But, dearest, I love still the same,
　　As when thy brow was fair,
When free from thought of sorrow's name,
　　Thou knewest naught of care,
And thou art still, though older grown,
　　My own, my dearest love,
And will remain, ever mine own,
　　Till call'd from earth, above.[1]

1　Written in Liverpool, 17th Dhulheggia 1324 (1st February 1907) and published in TC, Vol. XXIX, No.734, 6th February 1907, p.925.

THE LOVER'S PETITION I

Darling, could you know the passion,
　　　You have kindled in my breast,
Deep, profound, sincere and lasting,
　　　Not to be by words expressed,
You would then pity your lover,
　　　Cease to make him sigh and moan,
Try love, and you will discover,
　　　That his heart is all your own.

Oh! my darling, do have pity,
　　　Torture not a loving heart,
Think how happy we're together,
　　　How unhappy when we part.
Give this question your reflection.
　　　Picture years of joy and bliss,
And returning my affection,
　　　Give your answer in a kiss.[1]

1　Written in Liverpool, 4th Saphar 1325 (20th March 1907) and published in *TC*, Vol.XXIX, No.739. 20th March 1907, p.1022.

THE LOVER'S PETITION II

List, my darling, to my pleading,
Never mind the moments speeding,
'Tis thy lover that is speaking,
'Tis thy heart that he is seeking,
Longing e'en to touch thy finger,
Happy by thy side to linger,
Thinks thy voice like sweet birds humming
Joyful when he sees thee coming.

His love fix'd and never changing,
Mind from thee that ne'er goes ranging
Love so ardent, fierce and burning,
Difficulties ever spurning,
Passion fierce and all consuming,
Fearing naught and all presuming,
Hoping always and doubting never
Thee to gain and keep forever.[1]

---

1   Written on 21st Saphar 1325 (5th April 1907) and published in *TC*, Vol.XXIX, No.742. 10th
     April 1907, p.1065.

ODE TO THE MONTH OF MAY

We greet thee May,
Merry and gay,
With bright and sunny hours,
Sweet 'tis to stray,
At close of day,
Among thy dainty flowers.

The winter's dead,
On every bed
Are flow'lets bright and fair,
And chirp and song
Now float along
From warblers everywhere.

Above we view
The sky so blue
Just ting'd with burnish'd gold.
In meadows gay
The young lambs play,
Amidst the grazing fold.

Anon we hear
The streamlet clear,
Go rippling on its way;
The weary breast
It lulls to rest
So tender is its lay.

So while we live,
We'll ever give
A welcome to thee, May,
Thou art the queen,
O, month so green!
Thou lovely, smiling May.[1]

---

1   Written on 17th Rabia-al-awal, 1325 (1st May 1907) and published in *TC*, Vol.XXIX, No.746, 8th May 1907, p.1132.

THE MAIDEN AND THE PHILOSOPHER

"Now tell to me and tell me true
What is this thing called love by you;
Is it a fancy or a dream,
Flickering star or bright sunbeam,
To shine a while then pass away
A creature of a month or day,
That quickly comes, as quickly past.
Or is it something that doth last,
That once firm fix'd can never range,
That stands for aye and knows no change,
That has no doubt, is ever sure,
That until death doth firm endure.
That firm unites dear soul to soul
True as the needle to the pole
Strong as steel, secure as lock,
As firm as adamantine rock,
That bindeth one true heart to heart
In bonds so firm that none can part?"
So asked a maid with anxious eye,
And thus the savant made reply:
"True love for life is sunshine, light,
Our days on earth it maketh bright,
Unchanging, firm and free from strife,
It lasteth thus for aye through life."[1]

---

1   Written on 9th Jomada-as-sani, 1325 (20th July 1907) and published in *TC*, Vol.XXX, No.754, 3rd July 1907, p.12.

A MOTTO FOR LIFE

Never trifle with truth for a moment,
      But e'er keep a clear conscience within,
Be ye honest, and upright, and faithful,
      And give never a foothold to sin.
Thus be e'er true to your God and yourself.
      If in holiness you would ever grow,
To every enticement to evil
      Have the courage, dear friend, to say No.[1]

---

1   Written on 25th Jomada-al-awal 1325 (8th July 1907) and published in *TC*, Vol.XXX, No.756, 17th July 1907, p.41.

THE SONG OF THE WORKING GIRL

I am only a working girl,
     And I'm not ashamed to say
That I'm one of those who toil,
     For my living day by day.

With willing feet I trudge along,
     O'er the rugged paths I tread,
Happy that I have skill and strength,
     To thus earn my daily bread.

When I meet with a scornful sneer,
     Then I lift up my head with pride,
I know an honest working girl
     Can at all such sneers deride.

True-minded men well understand
     That the purest and brightest pearl
Of all the gems of womanhood
     Is an honest working girl.[1]

---

1   Written on 22nd Jomada-al-awal 1325 (5th July 1907) and published in *TC*, Vol.XXX, No.758., 31st July 1907, p.73.

WHAT IS LIFE?

What is our Life?
A breath, a moan, a sigh,
A laugh, a smile, a cry,
A storm, a sob, a calm,
Tumult, some joy, some harm.
An earthly moment brief,
That longs for some relief
And freedom from stern strife,
Such, ever such, our life![1]

1   Written in London, 10th Jomada-as-Sani 1325 (21st July 1907) and published in *TC*, Vol.XXX, No.759, 7th August 1907, p.91.

WHEN THOU ART NIGH

Bright shines the sky
When thou art nigh;
    Earth is a bower
    Bedeck'd with flower;
The hours glide by.
    There is no bliss
    Compares with this.
Happy the day
For all seems gay
When thou art nigh.

With thou not here
How dark and drear.
    This earth a tomb,
    Dismal and gloom;
The hours drag by,
    Each hour a day,
    When thou'rt away.
Dull aches my head,
Heavy as lead,
    With thee not nigh.

So speak, my dear,
My heart now cheer,
    And let me find
    Sweet solace kind
Within thy eye.
    And these words say
    That from this day
    That thou art mine
    And I am thine
    Until we die.[1]

---

1   Written on 1st Rajab 1325 (11th August 1907) and published in *TC*, Vol.XXX, No.760, 14th
    August 1907, p.104.

A LOVE SONNET

My darling, from your glistening eyes
Now give me that glance that I so much prize,
    That sets my heart aflame.
'Tis yours to give; on me bestow,
And let me feel before I go
    You are indeed my dame.

Be sure, my love, within my arms
Soft nestling there, with all your charms,
    You e'er will happy be.
Responsive then speak heart to heart;
Oh, may naught come that e'er can part
    Your loving soul from me.

In true love join'd, then side by side
Together through the world we'll glide,
    Dull care for ever gone.
And hand to hand, thro' life we'll go
Thro' paths of joy or paths of woe,
    United thus as one.[1]

---

1   Written on 1st Shaaban 1325 (9th September 1907) and published in *TC*, Vol.XXX, No.764. 11th
September 1907, p.168.

THE POET'S DREAM

I dreamt that I dwelt in a distant land,
    Where the sun shone bright each day,
And the air was sweet and with zephyr fann'd,
    And all seemed light and gay.
To me was joy and bliss and peace,
    And, standing there at my side
(My love for her will never cease),
    Was the one that I hailed as my bride.

It seem'd that the days sped bright and gay,
    And the skies were blue above;
And my bride and I as day followed day,
    Sweet basked in each other's love.
And I dreamt, oh, such a happy dream,
    That an angel had come from above,
And a fair babe lay, on a mother's knee,
    A pledge of our mutual love.

But, alas and alas! 'twas only a dream,
    And I woke at the dawning of day,
And instead of a ray of radiant beam,
    The skies were all sombre and gray.
But that dream doth lie in my memory still,
    And from there it ne'er will pass,
And I pray for the day, come when it will,
    When my dream will come to pass.

And every eve, as I lie on my bed,
    I long to dream once more,
And to be with her, 'neath that sun so red,
    Away on that distant shore.
And I fervently pray, to God each day,
    At morning and evening and noon
And my heart doth say, as I fervently pray,
    My prayer will be granted soon.[1]

---

1   Written on 21st Shaaban 1325 (1st October 1907) and published in *TC*, Vol.XXX, No.768, 9th October 1907, p.232.

GIVE ME THY HEART

Give now your heart to me!
    Yearning for thee am I;
To be with thee is ecstasy,
    Happy when thou art nigh.
Give then thy heart to me.
    Dearer than blooms that blow
    Where salt tides never flow.

Give me thy heart—thy pain
    If needs be, and thy stress;
Queen of my soul, there ever reign,
    Why stay in loneliness?
Give then thy heart to me.
    Then I shall be content,
    Happiness permanent.

Give to my heart that yearns
    Ever and all for thee
Now, when the old delight returns,
    Thy heart inviolably.
Give then thy heart to me.
    Why should'st thou still delay?
    Give me thy heart this day.[1]

---

1   Written on 13th Ramazan 1325 (20th October 1907) and published in TC, Vol.XXX, No.770, 23rd October 1907, p.269.

THE TWO ARCHERS

I saw an archer draw his bow,
    And send a keen thro' the air;
An arrow shot in careless sport
    To fall he cared not where.
It lighted 'mongst the ferns, and pierced
    A hart that bounded there.

I met thee on one fatal day,
    And on that day ere we did part
You shot a glance from your bright eyes
    That pierced me like a dart.
Oh lovely archer, pity me,
    Mine is the wounded heart![1]

---

1   Written on 15th Ramazan 1325 (23rd October 1907) and published in TC, Vol.XXX, No.771,
     30th October 1907, p.285.

UMAYMA

Umayma, my darling, now give me at last,
    The boon for which I have long hunger'd sore;
When groping blindly I meet with the blast
    That shipwreck'd my hopes on a rock-bounded shore.

As there for a time like a wreck on the strand
    I lay, and I thought with a sore bitter mind,
This life was a farce, ties mere ropes of sand,
    And love a mere name, or something of that kind.

But when I met *you*, then my soul then awoke,
    And I found then, my dear, a new object in life;
I could not keep silence, so those words I then spoke,
    And begged you, Umayma, to become my wife.

The words by me spoken I would not recall,
    Even though were I able to do;
I want you Umayma for ever and all,
    For I love, yes I only love you.

Cast aside all your doubts, fling away all your fears,
    And trust me by night and by day;
As long as I live, thro' all the long years,
    I'll love you for ever and aye.

So doubt not my love, for a moment ne'er think
    That to you I could inconstant be;
You've enthralled my heart 'till there is not a chink,
    That is not devoted to thee.

Umayma, my darling, be easy in mind,
    And sweet peace ever stay in your breast;
To you I'll be faithful and loving and kind,
    So now come to my arms and there rest.[1]

---

1   Quilliam claims to have translated the poem from the Arabic but does not provide details of the original source. He provides the following footnote: "Translator's note—the alterations in the rhythm of the verses is in agreement with the original lines in Arabic". Written on 6th Muharrum 1326 (7th February 1908) and published in *TC*, Vol.XXXI, No.786, 12th February 1908, p.109.

UMAYMA'S KISS

Sweet as the sweetest flower,
Grand as an eagle's flight,
Rich as a princely dower,
Strong as a hero's might,
True as a star above,
Is Umayma's kiss of love.

Pure as a snow-white soul,
Warm as the sun's bright ray,
Tender as the Zacat dole,
Bright as a summer's day,
There can be no greater bliss
On earth than Umayma's kiss.[1]

---

1 As with the previous poem also translated from the Arabic. Written on 9th February 1908 (6th Muharrum 1326) and published in *TC*, Vol.XXXI, No.790, 11th March 1908, p.174.

HAIL TO THE FOUNTAIN

Hail to thee, flowing waters;
     Hail to thee, crystal spring;
Come, listen, while our daughters
     Thy praises joyful sing.

Long may thy fair fame linger,
     Long may thy waters flow,
So chants each maiden singer,
     In rhythm sweet and low.

Flow on, thy waters springing,
     To fill the shady pool,
And health and comfort bringing,
     E'er with your waters cool.[1]

---

1   An example of a pre-Islamic "well song", translated from the Arabic was "rendered into English verse by the Sheikh", *TC*, Vol.XXXI, No.794, 8th April 1908, p.235.

OMAR WA UMAYMA
(OMAR'S REQUEST AND UMAYMA'S RESPONSE)

Omar's Request

Umayma, my darling, the joy of my heart,
To whose side I e'er haste and hate from to part;
A promise me give, that will give me delight
And give it me soon, aye, love, give it tonight.
Place your hand, then, in mine, and say for my life,
In future I'm yours, your own true loving wife.

Umayma's Response

Omar-bin-Hassan, why speak in this fashion?
Now is it true love, or is it but passion,
That puts coal to your lips and makes them outpour
Those words like a torrent to surge 'gainst the shore?
Now answer me truly, and then be content,
For silence is ever a maiden's consent.[1]

---

1   The final poem of the three translations from the Arabic describing the love of Omar and
    Umayma and the last of the poems to be published in *The Crescent*. The Sheikh would depart for
    Istanbul shortly after and the newspaper would cease publication. Written on 27th Saphar 1326
    (28th March 1908) and published in *TC*, Vol.XXXI, No.800, 20th May 1908, p.333.

THE TAKING OF THE GUNS AT MONS

It is of the British Lancers,
    The gallant "Ninth," I sing,
And to those sons of England brave,
    This little tribute bring,
And in verse now tell the story
    How gallant British sons,
At Mons, the Teuton put to rout
    And silenced, there, the guns—

'Leven cannon were in ambush
    And Germans there did lay,
Intent, with hellish iron hail,
    The British troops to slay;
The bugle sounded for the charge—
    The Lancers, with a smile
'Midst hail of shrapnel and of lead,
    Rode forward, a full mile.

Thro' infantry that barr'd their course,
    Fiercely they held their way.
In vain it was the Teuton tried
    Britannia's sons to stay;
Still on they rode, that gallant band
    Heroes of noble cause.
They reached their quarry, and there slew
    The Foe 'neath cannon's jaws.

The gunners slain, the guns made dumb
      (Not one was let remain),
Midst fire of rifle and of shell
      Rode they then back again;—
That deed shall live in ages yet,
      History's page upon.
Recorded e'er, the story there,
      Of that brave charge at Mons.[1]

---

1   The poem falls within the category of those celebrating heroic military deeds but does not proclaim Muslim bravery as in previous entries. In this poem, Quilliam, probably the first published under his new identity of H.M. Léon, demonstrates his patriotism and celebrates the charge of the Ninth Lancers at the Battle of Mons, Sunday, 23rd August 1914. *TP*, January 1915, pp.2–3; Russell Markland, *The Glory of Belgium, An Anthology* (London: Erskine MacDonald, 1915), p.64. He wrote the poem in early September at Paddington Train Station upon reading reports of the engagement (handwritten note by Léon in the Markland anthology with amendments to the printed poem, included above, p.64), ex-libris copy Charles Atwood Kofoid, with handwritten dedication to Dr Poole from the editor and poet, Robert Markland.

THE ROCK ON THE VOLGA

Hast heard of a rock on the Volga,
    A pillar that stands there alone,
The wild moss from base unto summit,
    Doth cover its grim walls of stone?

For ages that rock on the Volga,
    Hath stood with its crown ever bare,
The wind and the storm never heeding,
    And callous to pain and to care.

Up there on that rock on the Volga,
    On dizziest height of its crest,
The eagle, the fierce and mighty,
    Hath built there its eerie, its nest.

The crest of that rock on the Volga,
    The foot of but one man hath prest,
His name lives for e'er on the Volga:
    Stenka Razin, the hero, the blest.

One night up that rock on the Volga,
    He clamber'd its grim walls of stone,
And mused on the wrongs of the people,
    All silent he sat there alone.

When sun shone on rock on the Volga,
    Great deeds in his breast had been born,
His soul there he gave unto Freedom,
    All tyrants to hold e'er in scorn.

Down there from that rock on the Volga,
    Away from the sound of its wave,
He march'd that true son of the Volga,
    The people from tyrants to save.

Ne'er more to that rock on the Volga,
　　Did Stenka, the hero, return,
He yielded his life for the people,
　　The crown of a martyr did earn.

It stands there that rock on the Volga,
　　And rears still its crest o'er the wave,
And mutely it e'er tells the story,
　　On Stenka, the noble, the brave.

Stand firm still, oh rock on the Volga,
　　Heedless of the storm or the blast,
Proclaiming for ever this message,
　　That Freedom shall triumph at last.[1]

1　Based on an uprising led by Stenka (Stephen) Razin against Alex, Tsar of Russia (1645–76). Published as H.M. Léon, written on 23rd January 1915 and published in *The Philomath*, June 1915, pp.101–2.

THE SONG THAT LIVED

A poet once upon a time,
Did venture to essay a rhyme,
And to himself did amusing say,
"I'll sing a song to live for aye."
Then one he wrote to please the crowd,
They chorused it in accents loud;
It reign'd a month; and then, one day,
The crowd took up another lay.
"No more I'll write, vile mob, for you,"
He said, and wrote to please the few;
His song was sung before a king,
And then—became forgotten thing.
"Begone," he said, "all thought of self,
All thirst for fame, I'll please myself,
I'll pen a strain from such apart,
I'll write the thoughts within my heart."
His inmost thoughts, then he did pen,
Not caring he for king or men,
He sang of joy, he spoke of tears,
And lo! his song outliv'd the years.
The only song that ne'er knows death,
The one that e'er holds vital breath,
The lines that want no skill or art,
Are those, which gush forth from the heart.[1]

---

1   An important poem as the Sheikh returns to his identity as Quilliam and uses the theme of the
     poem to represent his feelings on the events of his life. The poem written for a king probably
     refers to the visit of the King to the Isle of Man. Signed as William Henry Abdullah Quilliam
     and written on the 26th December 1916, and published in *TP*, February 1917, p.52.

UNTITLED (1916A)

O Haggadah, strange work of bygone age,
With childish tale, yet wisdom of a sage,
At thy command, speech doth adorn the brute,
Thy essence, Truth, and wit thy attribute.
Naught frightens thee, and naught can bid thee stay,
Riddles thou solve, in thy unique own way.
For Israel, thou e'er be a star,
Shine on, bright one, shine on, O Haggadah![1]

---

1   Taken from H.M. Léon, *The Haggadah* (London: La Societé Internationale de Philologie,
    Sciences et Beaux-Arts, 1916), p.30. The Haggadah is the "story of the Exodus and redemption
    of the people of Israel by God, read during Passover services. Developed over centuries,
    it includes excerpts from the Bible, rabbinical writings, psalms, stories, and prayers," see
    "Haggadah", *Oxford World Encyclopedia* (Oxford: University Press, 2004).

YA HODJA! (OH TEACHER)

"Important 'tis," God's Prophet said, "to guide the infant mind,
By admonition kindly gi'en, and conduct firm yet kind.
A child is like a budding shrub, and thou wilt ever find,
Just as thou bendest tender twig, so is the tree inclined."
So Hodja watch conduct and word, when thou with children deal,
Let them not see the mere Hodja, but thou their *döstman* feel;[1]
Line upon line, step after step, thus serve instruction's meal,
Patience thy motto ever be, thy actions wisdom seal;
So when thy pupils, after, do, to manhood firm attain,
Whate'er success they gather then, thine also be the gain;
Thine was the hand, the infant mind, did so in order train,
That for their king, Wisdom they placed, within their mind to reign.
Oh Hodja! thine's a noble task, and if without a taint,
Thou dost thy duty cheerfully, and it ne'er shirk or feint,
Thou art a hero, noble, bold, such one as poets paint,
And Allah, thee, blessings will give, and count thee as a saint.[2]

1 *Döstman*, friend.
2 Henri M. Léon, *TP*, January 1917, pp.14–15. This poem and the one after next would appear to
follow the format of the poems that are attributed to the Sufi Haroun Abdullah, but are published
as written by Henri M. Léon, although the second poem is described as "translated from the
Turkish". These may have been rejected from the Haroun Abdullah collection and supports the
evidence that these poems were written by Quilliam sometime after 1908.

THE MOANING OF THE PINES

Lo I hear a sound as of deepest sighing,
    A sound in the trees, as of murmurings low,
A sound as one hears when some one is dying,
    A sound as of wind moaning over the snow.

Oh what is that sound, and what is it saying?
    Is it a message bearing sadness and gloom?
Is it the dull cry of Nature decaying,
    That thus, in the trees, sighs with piteous boom?

There now I hear it in doleful tones singing,
    So sadly singing in a doleful low tone,
Why do I hear it? Why will it keep ringing?
    Why do I fear it? Why doth it ever moan?

It sounds like a knell, yet ever complaining,
    Holds me with a spell, tho' I loathe to be hearing,
Ever a dull sound, and ever maintaining,
    Cry, sad and profound, a sound to be fearing.

Oh tell me ye wind, why thus ye are groaning?
    Tell me, oh be kind, and tell me, why ye sigh?
Ah! Now I perceive, 'tis dismally moaning,
    "To-day ye do live, but to-morrow ye die!"[1]

---

1   Henri M. Léon, 17th January 1917 published in *TP*, September 1917, pp.249–50.

YALNIZ (ALONE)

"Allah hath declared unto man 'Fear not, for I am with you, I will hear and I will see.'" Sura Ta Ha, Koran.[1]

Alone, doth man pass, when he endeth this life,
Alone, he endures its troubles and strife,
Alone, 'fore his God, to be judged at last,
Alone, must he bear the sentence then pass'd,
Alone, he to answer, for ev'ry misdeed,
Alone, then to prove his faith and his creed.
Alone, man retire, e'er it be too late,
Alone, then deep muse on thy possible fate,
Alone, then resolve for sin to atone,
Alone, man e'er strive. Yet, never alone;
For learn thou, O man! whatever betide,
Thou art not alone; God is by thy side.[2]

---

1 Sale, 46:10, p.308; directly echoing the King James Bible translation of *Isaiah* 41:10.
2 Henri M. Léon, written 22nd April 1917 described as "translated from the Turkish" and published in *TP*, September 1917, p.250.

THE SONG OF THE BROOK

When jaded, tired and feeling overwrought,
With languid eye, and dullness in the brain,
Turn thou from books, fresh vigour to regain,
And seek the ozone which the sea-wave brought,
Gaze into Nature, wander 'neath the trees,
List to the hum of insects in the air,
Hark to the song of birds and their joys share,
With fragrant perfume wafted on the breeze;
Behold the babbling brook and list its song,
See how it ripples over mossy stone,
Catch thou the message from its merry tone
As down the glen it gently flows along—
"Push on, fight on, sing on, and e'er rejoice,"
Warbles the brook to those who hear its voice.[1]

---

1   Written 24th July 1917, The Towers, Onchan, Isle of Man, as H. M. Léon, published in *TP*,
     October 1917, p.271.

AL-FAJR—THE DAYBREAK

I fly for refuge unto Allah, the Lord of the daybreak.
Sura 113, Al-Falaq, Koran.[1]

At Al-Fajr dawn, when sun doth out peep
　　From couch in the East, so dark and so dim,
I ope my eyes and awaken from sleep,
　　And softly murmur to Allah my hymn,
The words come quickly, so fervent and true,
　　Not strung together by method or art;
They harmonize there, as in rainbow hue,
　　For my tongue utters the cry of the heart;
"All glory to God, the Eternal One,
　　All praise be to Him, the Source of all light,
Who causeth the day, who hath fix'd the sun,
　　And granteth sweet sleep, when cometh the night."[2]

1　Sale, 113:1 (paraphrase), p.596.
2　Signed William Henry Abdullah Quilliam, Liverpool, 28th October 1917 and published in *TP*, November 1917, p.289.

1918

The old year has nigh reach'd its ending,
    Its hours are fast ebbing away;
Our thoughts to the New Year are tending,
    Leaving the old one to decay.

We trust that the new one is bringing
    To us neither sorrow nor fear,
And firm in our hearts there is clinging
    The wish for a Happy New Year.

To God, then, let each one be praying,
    With Faith, fervent, true and sincere,
That carnage may cease and end all slaying,
    And Peace reign within the New Year.[1]

---

1   Henri M. Léon, 23rd December 1917, published in *TP*, January 1918, p.16.

FIGHT ON

Be not dismay'd whate'er betide,
    Fight on! Fight on!
Do your best and patiently bide,
    Fight on! Fight on!

Thro' days of toil, tho' care assail,
    Fight on! Fight on!
The right is sure to yet prevail,
    Fight on! Fight on!

Let never doubt enter thy breast,
    Fight on! Fight on!
Be ever true and do thy best,
    Fight on! Fight on!

Tho' path be long, 'twill soon be past,
    Fight on! Fight on!
The victory will come at last,
    Fight on! Fight on![1]

---

1   Signed William Henry Abdullah Quilliam, 25 December 1911, and published in *TP*, January
    1918, pp.16–17, which is also biographically significant as it provides an emotional insight
    into Quilliam's state of mind during what might be called his years of crisis, 1908–13, see
    Introduction. Another poem where the poet reverts to his earlier identity even though he has
    adopted the Léon persona.

DEATH THE DAWN OF LIFE

Who speaks of Death, with hollow voice?
Waste not thy breath, rather rejoice?
Of toil and sorrow it the sunset is,
The Dawn of Morrow is Eternal Bliss.[1]

---

1   The quatrain is on the same page set directly above the following poem but is signed W.H.A.
    Quilliam.

SEVGHI SHIRKISI—A LOVE SONG

I think of thee at morning, I dream of thee at night,
When bright the sun is dawning and when dull fades the light;
I long for thee, my dear one, thy sympathy and love,
For when, dear, thou art near me, 'tis sunshine from above;
Blue the sky doth ever be, and always green the sea,
Paradise doth come to me when I am, love, with thee;
For thy love I only live, that love exist to gain,
To me, then, thy pure love give, let me it e'er retain;
Sweet one, Oh! close not thy heart, to this my earnest plea,
Sad my life, from thee apart, and rapture e'er with thee.[1]

---

1 Signed as Henri M. Léon, *TP*, February 1918, p.31, described by the poet as "From the Turkish"
but is likely to be his own composition, see Introduction.

A VALENTINE TO MY WIFE

Long years ago, so I have read,
    A saint on earth did dwell,
But where he liv'd, or what he said,
    That no one, now, can tell.

His holy name, Valentine be,
    And, when he went above,
Saint him they made, and patron he
    Of all, who truly love.

When second month the year doth greet,
    And fourteenth day arrive,
Each one should send, a missive sweet,
    To keep his fame alive.

Address'd this note must be, in chief,
    To one they love e'er true,
Therefore, you see, this poem brief,
    Dear wife, I send to you.

And with the verse, as you may guess,
    The wish, that God above,
Will keep, protect and ever bless,
    The one I truly love.[1]

---

1   Henri M. Léon, 14th February 1918, and published in *TP*, May 1918, p.72.

MUTALA‘A (REFLECTION)

I gazed upon the corn, one day, in autumn coloured hue,
Oh what a wealth of gold was there then spread before my view!
With what an open hand, indeed, does Allah gifts bestow,
The flow'rs that bloom, the birds who sing, the corn with golden glow;
Yet soon the grain 'neath sickle keen, upon the ground will lie,
So man, one day, must bow his head and yield his breath and die;
But as the grain is stored by man and kept for future need,
So Allah stores and record keeps of ev'ry well done deed.
The summer dies, the winter comes, swift past the seasons roll,
Withers the bud, the body dies, eternal is the soul![1]

---

1   Written 11th June 1918 and another example of a Turkish translation. The poet's note states: The
    word rendered "sickle" in the above translation, in the original is *tirpan*, which strictly speaking
    means "a scythe." The Turkish words for sickle are *orak, dass,* and *mishad*; the Arabic word *manjal*
    is also occasionally (but rarely) used. The above poem is sometimes headed *Taamul*, the Arabic
    word for "meditation" and "reflection". *Mutala'a* is the more correct Turkish term and is used
    by Ashiq Pasha, claimed to be the author of the poem (Henri M. Léon, *TP*, Sept–Oct 1918,
    pp.151–2).

THE 11TH NOVEMBER, 1918, AND AFTERWARDS

There's the clash of maroons banging,
There's the sound of bells a-clanging,
There are cries of exultation in the air;
Drums are beating, people cheering
At the good news, they are hearing,
That the War flame doth no longer lurid flare.

Females dancing, wildly, madly,
Children shouting, loudly, gladly,
Little wot they of the lives that are no more;
But I cannot join their madness,
For although 'tis day of gladness,
I well know that there are many hearts so sore.

There's a feeling o'er me creeping,
That I hear the women weeping
For the lives that naught can ever now restore,
There are maim'd men slowly dying,
There are cripples on beds lying,
That word VICTORY is written in men's gore.

Speak ye not of martial glory,
Tell me not the horrid story,
Stop that shouting, bid this revelry to cease;
'Tis unseemly all this yelling,
All man's better feelings quelling,
For it is unworthy *thus* to welcome peace.

Truth has triumph'd, glad I own it,
Shame has come to those who've sown it,
And their fiendish plans have all been brought to naught;
Do not then unseemly revel,
Keep your balance ever level,
Act ye worthy of the cause for which ye've fought.[1]

---

1   Written 14th November 1918 and published as Henri M. Léon, M.A., LL.D., F.S.P, in *TP*, Nov–Dec 1918, p.174.

HOW TO MAKE PARSNIP WINE

An Old Recipe in a New Setting

If you want to live in luxury,
And not be "stiff as starch,"
And yet be economical,
Your parsnips pluck in March;
Then boil their roots in water clear,
'Till they are soft as rain,
Then pour into a colander,
And thus the liquor strain;
To ev'ry gallon you have got,
Give pounds of sugar three,
Boil for three-quarters of an hour,
Then yeast add gingerly;
A little toast add with the yeast,
Then let the liquor stand
For full ten days before the feast,
(Stir each day by hand);
Then ask your friends to dine with you,
And when they come to dine,
They all, who drink, with one accord,
Will praise your parsnip wine.[1]

---

1   Henri M. Léon, *TP*, January–March 1920, p.29.

THE SECRET POTENT DRUG

Helen dropped into the wine, of which the soldiers drank, a certain secret drug, an antidote of grief and pain including oblivion to all ills—He who drinks of this mingled cup sheds not a tear the livelong day, were death to seize his venerated sire or her who gave him birth, or were the sword buried in the bosom of his brother or greatly loved sister, no tear would ever, even then, bedew his cheeks. Homer, *The Odyssey.*

There is a certain secret drug,
    Not known to me its name,
Which potent is beyond all ken,
    And mighty in its fame;
An antidote of pain it be,
    A duller it of grief,
Oblivion grants to ev'ry ill,
    To all it gives relief.
For he, who quaffs this mingled cup,
    Would never shed a tear,
If death did seize his aged sire,
    And stretch him on a bier;
Nay, even if the one who bore
    And gave to him his birth,
Had ceas'd to breathe and now, once more,
    Was mingl'd with the earth;
Nor if the brother that he lov'd,
    Or sister he adored,
Had, cruel fate, their breast transfix'd
    With ruthless spear or sword.
This potent drug, in mystic jar,
    Doth Somnos ever keep,
And minute drops, in eyes doth place,
    And thus induces sleep.
How 'tis prepared I cannot say,
    But, when the moon be full,
Then certain plants of potent power
    'Tis requisite to pull;

From them, distill'd with mystic charm,
    In whispers scarcely heard,
At dead of night, midst bats and owls,
    The drug is then prepar'd.[1]

---

1   Henri M. Léon, *TP*, Oct–Dec 1920, p.92. Possibly an allegory for Islam or even the esoteric elements of Sufism.

AL-MIRAJ

"Prophet of God! I pray reveal the plan,
Which will produce such blessed state for man,"
Muhammad smiled, and then in accents clear,
Spake he these words, "Brother, have thou no fear,
This world and all can be for ever blest,
If men will learn to value what is best,
And learn to strive, not for themselves alone,
But each for all, and all for ev'ry one,
Then on the earth, aye on this very ground,
Peace then shall reign, and Paradise be found,
When in the world, all o'er land and sea,
Men shall be men, and men shall brothers be."[1]

---

1   H.M. Léon, *The Psychology of Oriental Peoples* (London: no pub., 1926), p.19, slightly amended
extract from H.M. Léon, "Al-Miraj", *SHA*, p.60.

PART 2

Sheikh Haroun Abdullah
A Turkish Poet and His Poetry
(1916)

From the Introduction

UNTITLED (1916B)

Full many a gem of purest ray serene,
    The dark unfathomed caves of ocean bear,
Full many a flower is born to blush unseen,
    And waste its sweetness on the desert air.[1]

---

1   *SHA*, Preface, p.12. In reference to the largely untranslated treasures of Turkish and particularly Ottoman literature.

RIJA SHAIRIN (THE POET'S PRAYER)

Oh, Allah! grant to me to speak in fiery song,
That I may sternly brand all falsehood, vice and wrong,
So 'gainst them I can strive in words of blazing fire,
And longings for the truth e'en all the world inspire,
My voice as lightning strike, as thunder loud and clear,
With burning pregnant words, resounding and sincere,
My soul longs, Allah, ever thus to work for Thee;
It only wants the strength; *that*, Allah give to me.[1]

---

1   Introduction, *SHA*, p.21, described as Sheikh Haroun Abdullah's first poem.

HABEEBA

Habeeba dear to me, thy image fills my soul,
The thought of thee inflames, and burneth like a coal;
My love for thee is, oh! so great, its pleasure gives me pain,
And when I try thee to forget I only try in vain;
A single glance from thy sweet eye enthralls me with a spell,
Thy lips do with the rosebud vie, and honey there doth dwell.
Thy raven tresses, black as jet, like ebony do shine,
Thy voice as soft as cooing dove, or nightingale divine;
Thy pearly teeth, rich gems they be, as those from depths of sea,
The sweetest peach or nectarine is not so sweet as thee;
The sight of thee intoxicates far more than ruby wine;
Habeeba, love, my darling one, oh say that thou'lt be mine.[1]

---

1   Introduction, *SHA*, pp.22–3. See discussion in the Introduction to this volume.

BIRTHDAY POEM/RUZGAR SHARKI
(THE WIND SONG)

Though bitter blow the raging storm,
  And years pass on in flight,
Allah preserve thee from all harm,
  And make this new year bright!
May all the blessings God can give
  Upon thy head descend,
In happiness may thou long live,
  And peaceful be thy end.

Cold blows the blast, the wind moans sad and drear,
The sky's o'ercast; my husband is not here!

Sevgilim,[1] tell me now, without delay,
How blows the wind upon my peach to-day?

Soft blows the wind and Zephyrs gently glide,
With balmy breath; my husband's at my side.
Sing now, ye birds, and murmur soft, O wind!
Enthralled in love, I ev'ry pleasure find.[2]

---

1 *Sevgilim*, my beloved. Recourse has been made to Quilliam/Léon's own translations by reference
  to the glossary he provided (Glossary, *SHA*, pp.95–103); further explanatory glosses in round
  brackets have been added where necessary.
2 Introduction, *SHA*, pp.24–5. A dialogue between Sheikh Haroun and his beloved Habeeba,
  with the first exchange called "Birthday Poem" occurring while they were parted. The Sheikh
  then seeks the Sultan's permission to leave court to return home, which is granted. Their second
  exchange, called "*Ruzgar Sharki* (The Wind Song)", takes place when the Sheikh arrives home.

ESSEFLER (REGRETS)

A bunch of flowers now lay upon her tomb,
Love's still fond homage to the dead one there;
And as thou sittest lone within thy room,
And tears fall silent, offer then thy prayer,
That thou, by deeds of love, may heaven attain,
And meet, when there, the lov'd one once again;
And when thy prayer be ended, then review,
As in a vision, limn'd in colours true,
The dear one's life, its oft and bitter pain,
Her sufferings here, *Al-Jannat*[1] to attain;
All that is o'er, her troubles at an end,
(May Allah us sweet consolation send!)
That faithful heart shall never more be wrung,
Her praises now the theme for poet's tongue;
No cold neglect to give her aching care,
Her's now the bliss, our portion the despair;
Too late regrets, too late forgiveness e'en to crave,
Nought left, except to mourn, and shed tears o'er her grave.[2]

---

1   *Al-Jannat*, literally, the Garden; Paradise.
2   Introduction, *SHA*, p.27. This poem is depicted as composed by Sheikh Haroun twenty years
    after Habeeba's premature death expressing his undimmed grief; he sends the poem to his only
    son Ahmad (also the name of Quilliam's oldest son, Robert Ahmed Quilliam (1879–1954)).

RĀSIKH SEV (ENDURING LOVE)

I'll pen a song, a chant of love,
 Of one I ne'er forget,
When but a boy, she was my joy,
 And oh, I love her yet!

Long years have flown, I've older grown,
 And other maids I've met,
But from my heart she ne'er doth part,
 For oh, I love her yet!

Her eyes so blue, her heart so true,
 My own, my darling pet,
Her cheery voice, my young heart's choice,
 I hear,—and love her yet.

Tho' in the mould, her form lies cold,
 With stone above her set,
My heart doth say, she lives to-day,
 And oh, I love her yet!

I have no fear, that sometime near,
 When we again have met,
We both will say, that joyous day,
 Dear one, I love thee yet![1]

---

1   Introduction, *SHA*, p.28. This poem is depicted as written by Sheikh Haroun for Habeeba
    towards the end of his life, in which he anticipates a heavenly reunion with his beloved.

MUSSĀLĀHĀ (PEACE)

Allah inviteth you into the dwelling of Peace.
Younus, Sura 10, Koran[1]

Grant, Thou, oh Allah! this my pray'r
Upon the earth, that ev'rywhere
Mankind may with each other bear,
And lead a peaceful life;
That they may truly Islam know,
More like thy Prophet daily grow,
And live together here below,
In love and not in strife.

Oh, Allah! who doth all things know,
Who sent Thy Prophet here to show
How mankind could the better grow,
And strife and tumult cease;
Oh, Allah! hear me when I pray,
That thou wilt speedy send the day
When men shall cease to war and slay,
And shall abide in peace.[2]

---

1   Sale, 10:25 (paraphrase), p.202.
2   Introduction, *SHA*, pp.30–1; also in Léon, "Life and Poetry of Sheikh Haroun Abdullah", *Asiatic Review*, p.435; purportedly one of Sheikh Haroun's poems in exile.

CHOJUQLIQ (CHILDHOOD)

How sweet it is to be a child, and live but for the hour,
To sport like *parvan*[1] in the sun, and glide from flow'r to flow'r,
To sit beside the running stream, and hear its murmuring song,
To have a heart as feather light, with ne'er a thought of wrong,
To feel the balmy breath of spring and catch the rainbow's hue,
And with a merry dancing step to brush away the dew,
To watch the *Chèsmé*[2] merry splash and clutch its diamond spray,
To sleep contented every night and only dream of day;
Oh! for those days of *Chojuqliq*, those happy, happy hours,
When the day was bright with sunshine, when life was gay with flowers,
As time went on they vanished, again ne'er to return,
Experience may bring wisdom, but sorrow, too, we learn.
It is not joy that doth increase with ever growing years,
But anxious cares and troubles sore, sorrows and many tears;
So now me tell, and truly tell, you thoughtful thinking men
Would not ye be more happy now, a child to be again?[3]

---

1   *Parvan*, a butterfly.
2   *Chèsmé*, a fountain.
3   Introduction, *SHA*, pp.31–2; purportedly one of Sheikh Haroun's poems in exile.

EFENDIMIZ! RABBINEZ-TA-ALA!
(LORD OF US ALL! OUR EXALTED MASTER!)

To Thee, O Allah! Praise will I for ever sing,
The joyful tribute of my heart to Thee I bring,
My yearning soul to know Thee doth for ever strive,
In close communion with Thee to arrive,
I long to dwell beneath the shadow of Thy arm,
Thy Holy Name to me will ever be a charm,
I long to soar to Thee, to be with Thee above,
Thy Majesty o'erpow'rs, my heart yearns for Thy love;
I chant Thy greatness, tho' Thyself I never see,
Thou art the only One, nought there exists like Thee;
Thy Holy Messenger in words of Truth and Light,
Did tell all of Thy glory, all pervading, bright,
The more I heard of Thee, the more I sought to know,
That nearer thus to Thee I might for ever grow.[1]

---

1   Introduction, *SHA*, p.33. Portrayed as a poem Sheikh Haroun wrote on his return to court at the
     suggestion of a courtier, who suggested that he write a laudatory ode to further gain the pleasure
     of the Sultan. Ignoring the unctuous courtier, the Sheikh wrote the poem "*Effendimiz*" in praise
     of God. The Sheikh's exile had purportedly ended when the Sultan, Murad IV, had been pleased
     by another of the Sheikh's poems written in exile that honoured the Sultan's forefather, Ertoghrul
     (Introduction, *SHA*, pp.32–3).

KUGHUK-KUSHU (THE CUCKOO)

It happ'd one day in foreign clime,
 Now full five years ago,
(The month of April was the time),
 My heart was full of woe;
Misfortune 'pear'd to dog my feet,
 All seem'd of dismal hue,
When lo! From green-leaf'd sweet retreat,
 I heard the cry, "Cuckoo!"
  "Cuckoo! Cuckoo!"

Ah! errant wand'rer art thou there,
 And to thy mate dost sing,
Dost thou a message to me bear,
 Thy heralder of spring?
Hast now the winter truly sped,
 For me and Nature, too,
Will I now wake, as from the dead?
 The bird replied, "Cuckoo!"
  "Cuckoo! Cuckoo!"

I felt the bird a message bought,
 Of hope to weary heart,
It bade me strive, and fear for nought,
 Its song said, "Do thy part."
I left the spot, and turn'd me round,
 Fortune once more to woo,
Encouraged by that cheerful sound,
 The sweet bird's cry, "Cuckoo!"
  "Cuckoo! Cuckoo!"

I fought, I strove to conquer fate,
　　All obstacles o'ercame,
Early I rose and work'd till late,
　　To once more make a name;
I work'd, I pray'd, God heard my prayer,
　　And gave the answer too,
I know 'twas He, who in wood there,
　　Had bade bird cry, "Cuckoo!"
　　　　"Cuckoo! Cuckoo!"

"Praise be to God!" To Him all praise!
　　To Him all praise belong,
Who guideth men by wondrous ways,
　　Who gave the birds their song;
Who leadeth man by paths unseen,
　　Directs them what to do,
And sends to cheer, the springlet's queen,
　　With blithesome note, "Cuckoo!"
　　　　"Cuckoo! Cuckoo!"[1]

1　Introduction, *SHA*, pp.34–6. This poem is said to have pleased the Sultan so much that he ordered it "written in gold and placed in the Imperial Library" (Introduction, *SHA*, pp.33–4).

UYQU VÉ QARDISHANI ULUM
(SLEEP AND HIS BROTHER DEATH)

Upon the just dawn'd world, the new-born infant opes[1] its eye,
In wonderment, to gaze on what before it there may lie,
Then weary of the sight, e'en tho' it be but e'en a peep,
Doth nestle on its mother's bosom calmly there to sleep,

The weary toiler from his work thro' hours that long did seem,
Exhausted, tired, and with his senses in a clouded dream,
With heavy limbs, dull brain, and eyes that open cannot keep,
To find sweet solace from his toil doth lay him down to sleep,

A pilgrim thro' the world, unheeding there its gifts or sneer,
I pass along the road, whose milestones mark, each one, a year,
Waiting the time when Allah shall, in mercy, call my breath,
And give me rest and peace in the calm tranquil sleep of death.[2]

---

1   Ope: transitive verb, "to open", now poetic and English regional usage only, *OED*, 3rd Edn.
2   Introduction, *SHA*, p.37; also in Léon, "Life and Poetry of Sheikh Haroun Abdullah", *Asiatic Review*, p.436; it is said to have been written in the last few days of Sheikh Haroun's life.

Mystic Poems

NUR-ULLAH (THE LIGHT OF GOD)

In all great Allah's creatures, which in air, or sea, or ground,
In coldest or in warmest clime, where any life be found,
Most perfect of them all art thou, if thou wilt think, O man!
And can become, as 'twas designed in mighty Allah's plan,
The King of nature, perfect, true, onward to ever go,
E'er gaining knowledge as you speed, and to perfection grow;
First, thou must learn to know thyself, the only *tarik*,[1] this,
To learn of Allah, the true path to everlasting bliss.
For until thou dost know thyself, how cans't thou ever know,
He who the key of knowledge is, and can the pathway show?
But when thou dost thyself right learn, and comprehend the true,
Then Allah will Himself reveal, and be at one with you.
Did'st ever see the blazing sun reflected in the sea?
Did'st ever think what 'twas thou saw, what 'twas then seen by thee?
'Twas not the sun in sea thou saw, but 'twas reflected light;
That blaz'd and shone before thy gaze, so brilliant and so bright.
Reflected yes, but learn, O man! it was the *very* light,
None other than the light itself, that was before thy sight.
God is the Light, the Very Light, the Only One, the True!
Bask in that Light, secure that Light, let it e'er shine in you.
Thy attributes, oh, mark them well! for man they are divine,
Thy substance did from Allah come, 'tis His and yet 'tis thine—
And yet a difference doth exist, 'twixt Allah, Great, and thee,
A *casual* being, but thou art; *Essential,* Allah be.
Strive on, then, to perfection gain, and when this task be done,
No longer mere man wilt thou be, thou art with Allah—One.[2]

---

1   *Tarik*, path (to God).
2   Mystic Poems, *SHA*, pp.41–2. Depicted as one of Sheikh Haroun's Mevlevi teaching poems,
    distilling a commentary upon the Verse of Light (Quran 24:35) and the saying attributed to
    Imam Ali, "He who knoweth his own self, knoweth Allah." (Introduction, *SHA*, pp.20–1.)

TAMSIL (THE ANALOGY)

Come man and contemplate upon thyself and One,
Who was and ever is, whose day will ne'er be done.
Steadfast for Truth seek thou, and seek till it appear,
And know ye that the Truth no rival hath nor peer;
Seek thou within, seek thou without, seek thou alway,[1]
Till in thy very soul doth come its burning ray.
How foolish be the man, who on a darksome night,
Doth seek to find the sun by aid of candle-light;
But greater fool be he, who in the light of day,
Seeks for the mid-day sun by aid of torch's ray:
Now be thou not a fool, this *tamsil* then apply,
And learn a lesson thou, from self, from earth, from sky!
First then regard this globe then gaze upon the dome
In which the orb of day doth there for ever roam,
And yet it roameth not, for in the trackless sky
It ever standeth firm, 'tis *thou* that passeth by;
And yet it ever moves with no uncertain speed,
And passes on thro' space, as Allah hath decreed:
A fragment but it be of one harmonious whole,
A fragment equal be, oh man, thy very soul!
If sun alway stood still and never once did move,
And fixèd ever was in never changing groove,
Who it would ever know, who e'er would feel its beams,
Who could discern the light which ever from it gleams?
It ever burns and burns, yet not itself consumes,
Thy soul goes on for aye, and divers[2] forms assumes,
The babe, the boy, the man, are they not still one whole?
Outward they show a change, yet, but contain one soul.
Life emanates from One, to One returns again,
The Life and Light to One, to One alone pertain.
Light is Life, Truth is Life, and Light and Truth are one,
Life it doth never end, and never is begun.
Perfect Life is *the* Light, to *that* do thou attain,
In that Light, find thou Life, that Light e'er to retain.[3]

---

1   Alway: now mainly archaic and regional form of "always", *OED* 3rd Edn.
2   Divers: adj., obsolete form of "diverse" since 1700, *OED* 2nd Edn.
3   Mystic Poems, *SHA*, pp.43–4.

DĀȲMĀ QAPALI QAPASS (THE EVER-CLOSED DOOR)

There is a door to which I've found no key,
There is a veil thro' which I cannot see,
Much talk, much toil and speculation free
There is, and then—the end of thee and me.

'Tis strange, yet true, of many myriads, who
Have pass'd, long since, that door of darkness thro',
Not one has come to tell to me, to you,
The road o'er which we have to travel too.

They lived as we, like us they toil'd and tried
To solve the question (as there was no guide),
What in the future did for them betide,
They only found it—after they had died.

Why waste your time, in speculation vain?
The Present's thine, the Future, yet to gain;
Act now your part, and let the rest remain,
Till door do ope never to close again.[1]

---

1   Mystic Poems, *SHA*, p.45. Sheikh Haroun is depicted as being influenced by the Rubáiyát of
    Omar Khayyam, quatrains 32, 65, and 66 (Introduction, SHA, pp.21–2). However, Quilliam's
    opening verse is a direct lifting of the first edition (1859) of Edward Fitzgerald's translation of
    the thirty-second quatrain with minor amendments:
    There was a Door to which I found no Key:
    There was a Veil past which I could not see:
    Some little Talk awhile of ME and THEE
    There seem'd—and then no more of THEE and ME.
    Daniel Karlin remarks that "[i]n the early twentieth century the poem was spoken of as one of
    the two or three best-known in the English-speaking world", see E. Fitzgerald, *Rubáiyát of Omar
    Khayyam*, ed. Daniel Karlin (Oxford: University Press, 2009), pp.xi, 32.

TEFTISH (THE QUEST)

From all the world I turn, and all within it blind,
An ever constant joy, away from it to find.
The world I cast aside, its pleasures and its pain,
Its pain affects me not, its pleasures are all vain,
Where must I then now seek, to what direct my mind,
The object of my quest, to find and then to bind,
I gaze upon the sky, behold there clear and bright.
The mighty orb of day, the lesser ones of night,
I see some wax and wane, others that constant be.
And far beyond my ken, are orbs I cannot see;
Who fix'd those orbs in space, who gave them each their laws,
Who bade them shine as this, What is that Great First Cause,
That Architect Divine, Designer of the plan,
Of Firmament so vast, scarce realised by man?
No chaos there doth reign and discord is unknown,
Perfection reigneth there, Symmetry there is shown,
No flaw can there be found, in Unity they stand,
And testimony give, mute, yet supremely grand,
That One Almighty One, e'er near and yet afar,
Created moon and sun, planet and distant star,
This they do e'er proclaim, from time till time be done,
'Twas Allah made us all, and Allah is but One,
If Allah made them all, sure then it must be true,
That Allah all things made, and Allah made *me too,*
If made by Allah, then of Allah I am made,
To Allah to return, should I then be afraid?
Rather should I with glee endeavour to attain,
To such a happy state, and that result to gain,
So that in harmony with all creation be,
In one eternal whole, with Allah then in me;
Alone no longer then, will I be let remain,
If oneness with Allah, I can for ever gain,
This then shall be my goal, the prize to be e'er won,
With Allah e'er to be, and be with Allah, One.[1]

---

1 Mystic Poems, *SHA*, pp.46–7.

QARGHA (THE CROW)

Bird whose hue is black as jet,
Nest on high so firmly set,
Who your call can e'er forget?
                        Qargha! Qargha!

Bird with solemn thoughtful mind,
Holding conclave with your kind,
Sentries set, before, behind,
                        Qargha! Qargha!

Marching forward in close rank,
Rang'd upon the meadow bank,
Cornfield dry, or swamp so dank,
                        Qargha! Qargha!

Flying proudly in the sky,
Watching all both far and nigh,
Giving forth thy warning cry,
                        Qargha! Qargha!

Tell me now who is your King,
Do you to him tribute bring,
Why is it you ever sing?
                        Qargha! Qargha!

What's your creed, is't new or old?
Methinks birds so grave and bold,
Are within the Sufi fold.
                        Qargha! Qargha!

Harsh thy cry, yet ever clear,
Yet perchance in comrade's ear,
'Tis a sound the heart to cheer.
                        Qargha! Qargha!

Bird, from thee I'll lesson learn,
To grave matters, my mind turn,
Allah's approbation earn.

Qargha! Qargha![1]

1   Mystic Poems, *SHA*, pp.48–9.

AWARÉ (THE WANDERER)

A wanderer in the darkness seeking for path and light,
With willing heart and yearning mind yet groping in the night,
I cry "O Allah, Hear my cry, Oh guide me now aright,
Open Thou my eyes, inspire my mind, and quicken Thou my sight,
Give me the strength, the power, the will, to do what may be done,
To tread the way, the markèd path, as doth a planet run,
Along the course that Thou hast fixed its circle round the sun.
Complete, O Allah, now the work within my heart begun,
Teach me to build, upon sure base, a temple fair to see,
A house of pray'r, a place of rest, to e'er unspotted be,
A palace grand, for greatest King, a temple, Lord, for Thee,
And for its site, here in my heart, Allah, Oh let it be."[1]

---

1   Mystic Poems, *SHA*, p.50.

SUĀL (THE QUERY)

Who doth require a guide to show him o'er the ground,
When he himself, alone, the *tarik*, true hath found?
Who water needs to seek, when he hath found the fount?
Who ladder doth require to aid him there to mount,
When he doth surely stand on highest point of ground?
Who asks other for help, when answer true hath found?
Who seeks another's aid, his praises oft to sing,
When he himself doth bask in favour with his King?
'Tis thus the Dervish sits, when he his task hath done,
And out of self, himself, in Allah then is one.[1]

---

1   Mystic Poems, *SHA*, p.51.

RIJA (THE ENTREATY)

With opened eyes, I pass towards the Light,
With willing heart, I yearn to do the right;
But day is clothed with burdens of the night.

With opened eyes, I look towards the sun,
Then bend to toil at some good task begun,
To be destroy'd, e'er day its course hath run.

With opened eyes, I build, and then I see,
The building dedicated unto Thee,
Destroy'd, and yet 'twas beautiful to me.

With yearning soul, I long for peace and rest,
To cast the dross and treasure; all that's best,—
To find, at eve, my soul with doubts o'erpast.

Thy ways, Allah, I cannot comprehend,
But this I know, whether Thou break or mend,
All will be right when I attain the end.

Rija, I make O Allah, e'er to Thee,
Thy mercy, Allah, Oh bestow on me,
And open my blinded eyes that I may see.[1]

---

1   Mystic Poems, *SHA*, pp.52–3.

EMNIYYET (CONFIDENCE)

Vain and deceitful hopes are fit for none but senseless mind,
    Omens are superstitions vile, and dreams make fools rejoice,
Eager they grasp at shadows vain, eager they chase the wind,
    Eager consult the *faldji*,[1] they, and hang upon his voice,
What dolts they are, what fools they be, who in the *faldji* trust,
    Know not they that to God alone the future but is known,
'Fore Allah we but atoms be, contemptible as dust,
    Yet He doth watch and guide our path, and claims us for His own.
Trust not in man, but trust in God, the *Forkan*[2] be your guide,
    Therein is writ in pregnant words, all need by man be known,
Reveal'd by angel, incorrupt, preserv'd whate'er betide,
    Rest then in Islam, safety find, and trust in God alone.[3]

---

1   *Faldji*, a fortune-teller.
2   *Forkan* (*Furqān*), the Koran; more precisely, a name of the Quran, meaning "The Criterion (between right and wrong)".
3   Mystic Poems, *SHA*, p.54. This poem is sometimes termed *Eminliq*, "Security" (Author's footnote).

Historical Poems

PAYGHAMBAR VE YAHUDI
(THE PROPHET AND THE JEW)

Some there be, who hasty are, and heed not what they say,
Others think before they speak, and evil keep at bay,
To all of such, where'er they be, a story old and true,
Of what God's prophet did and said, e'en now I'll tell to you;
It chanced among the Sahaba[1] there, one day the prophet sat,
Abu Huraira too was there, likewise his friend, the cat,
Omar and Othman too were there, Ever their names blest!
And Abu-Bekr, wise and bold, sat there among the rest;
Ali, God's lion, foremost he, for ever in the fray,
Scholars and warriors, mighty men, were present on that day;
Attentive they, that in their minds, they thus could treasure well,
The words they heard, like precious pearls, which from the prophet fell;
But while they sat with list'ning awe, lo, there across the square,
With measured tread, some mourners came, it was a corpse they bore,
Straightway the prophet ceased his speech, his utterances so good,
And as the bier did pass him by, respectful, Ahmed stood.
"Rasul-Allah!"[2] then one did say, "why dost thou stand so here,
Know not thou, it is but a Jew, whose corpse lies on yon bier?"
The prophet turn'd, and as he turn'd, light flashing from his eye,
In accents clear, yet soft and low, 'twas thus he made reply:–
"That 'tis the corpse of a poor Jew, brother, I know full well,
But what of that, a Jew's a man, who on this earth doth dwell,
He hath a soul, immortal, that for eternal time,
Will still live on, to dwell for aye, in its appointed clime;
From that Jew's life, from that Jew's fate, we should example take,
And copy all was in him good, the evil e'er forsake,
As once liv'd he, so now we live, and in our time must die,
And stark and stiff, like yonder Jew, upon a bier must lie,
'Tis not for us, weak mortals we, the Jew's faith to deride,
That is for Allah's wisdom and His mercy to decide;
For us it is, to follow that, Allah has pointed clear,

---

1   Sahaba, the Prophet's Companions, correcting Quilliam's use of "Saheeb".
2   Rasul-Allah, Messenger of God.

Our *tarik* is in Islam's fold, rest there and have no fear,
And judge ye not your fellow man, but to yourself be true,
And leave to Allah's mercy, thou, the Christian and the Jew."[3]

---

3   Historical Poems, *SHA*, pp.57–8. While attributed to Sheikh Haroun who was said to have
    written it in 1610 (Introduction, *SHA*, p.29), the poem was published earlier as "By our
    esteemed brother H. Mustafa Henri Marcel Léon, Ph.D, LL.D, F.S.P.", see "The Prophet and the
    Jew. A poem.", *IR* (Woking), February 1915, pp.73–4.

ACRIMU-AL-HIRRAH! (RESPECT THE CAT)

Hast heard the story, how one summer's day,
Within a mosque, a cat once hapt to stray,
Just at the time God's prophet had gone there,
To make, as was his wont, the Zuhar[1] prayer?
With measur'd tread, it step'd with noiseless feet,
And, 'fore God's prophet, calmly took its seat,
And purring gently, sat there calm and still,
Afraid of nought, suspicious of no ill,
When lo! by Allah's will, e'er wise and good,
The cat was seiz'd, with pains of motherhood,
And 'twixt its pangs, common to all of earth,
There in the mosque, to kittens three gave birth.
"Remove the brute," then loudly one did cry,
"To thus pollute the mosque, sure it should die."
"Say not such words," God's prophet then did say,
"Remove it not, in peace let it here stay,
Do not a thing, its feelings now to jar,
Respect the cat, *Acrimú-al-hirrah*!
This cat hath only done, that which it should,
And hath performed its work of motherhood,
What Allah hath decreed for all the race,
As Nature's law, sure can be no disgrace;
And Muslims learn from this the lesson, that
Allah doth teach to all, Respect the cat!
Thy father honour, and thy brother love,
Protect thy sister, but of all above,
Respect thy mother, she it was who bare
Thee in her womb, and lavished on thee care
Known but to Allah; Muslims think of that,
This cat a mother is, Respect the cat!"[2]

1 Midday Prayer.
2 Historical Poems, *SHA*, pp.59–60. While attributed to Sheikh Haroun who was said to have written it in 1610 (Introduction, *SHA*, p.29), the poem was published earlier as "By our esteemed brother H. Mustafa Henri Marcel Léon, Ph.D, LL.D, F.S.P.", see "Acrimu-al-Hirrah!—Respect the cat. A poem.", *IR* (Woking), December 1914, pp.546–7.

KUDŪM ERTOGHRUL (THE COMING OF ERTOGHRUL)

Osmanlis gather round me, your attention I'll engage,
And now recite, in brief, to you, what's writ on Nischri's page;[1]
A story old, of warriors bold, a story that is true,
Of what your race, did do of grace against a Mongol crew.
'Twas 'bout six hundred years, or so, from time the Prophet fled,
From wicked men, who, curs'd, had placed a price upon his head;
A little band of Oghouz Turks, came wand'ring thro' the land,
Four hundred and just forty-four, was number of their band,
Down the Euphrates vale they came, with flocks and herds and tent,
Until they reach'd Angora's plain, so far by Allah sent,
They'd travelled far, o'er hill and vale, aweary all were they,
When coming thro' a rugged pass, a plain before them lay;
Oh! what a sight did meet their eyes, spread there before their view;
A battle fierce was being fought, betwixt a motley crew;
A horde of Mongols fierce and grim, with cries so loud and fierce,
Were beating back a little band, whose ranks they tried to pierce;
In vain the chief, who led that band did strive with might and main,
'Gainst horde of those, who were his foes, his foothold to maintain;
In vain his sword, did flash and gleam, in vain his warriors led,
For much outnumbered lo they were ('tis so by Nischri said)
For every foe, his good sword slew, ten more did seem to rise,
Like fabled snake of Hydra head and thousand gleaming eyes,
On, on they came, the Mongol horde, against his ranks they press,
Each moment sees a foeman fall and sees his ranks grow less,
"Oh Allah! hear a Muslim's call, Hear now a Muslim's cry,
Send aid, Oh Allah!, now to me, ere all my men do die!"
Scarce had the pray'r, 'scaped from his lips, scarce had it reached on high,
When Ertoghrul, Right-hearted man, and all his men drew nigh,
They saw the fray, the shouts they heard, beheld the desp'rate plight
Ala-ud-deen and his brave men, out-number'd in the fight,
Then out spake the Right-hearted man, "God's prophet said of old,
To aid the weak a duty is, so Muslims now be bold,
And follow me into the fray, succour that little band,
Which 'gainst exceeding powerful odds, so gallantly doth stand!"

---

1 "Nischri" died before 926H/1520CE, see C. Woodhead, "Neshri", *EI2*, Vol.8, pp.7–8. He
   wrote an important chronicle of early Ottoman history that helped to define the genre, see
   V.L. Menage, *Neshri's History of the Ottomans: The Sources and Development of the Text* (London:
   Oxford University Press, 1964).

His warriors then did grasp their spears, and to their horse gave rein,
And on the foe they rushed like wind, yea, like a hurricane,
The Mongols felt their spears keen point, which soon was stainèd red,
As Ertoghrul and his brave men like whirlwind on them sped;
They reel, they feint, their ranks give way, they turn their backs and flee,
As doth a ship in sorry plight, before a raging sea.
Amaz'd the Seljuk Sultan stands to see the havoc wrought,
Upon his foes, by heroes bold, the men by heaven brought,
The blows they smite, the deeds they do, upon him he doth gaze,
And more he looks and more he sees the greater his amaze;
"Can they be men or angels they, like those on Bedr's field,[2]
Who fought for Islam's heroes there and made the kaffirs yield?"
When lo a cry, "Allah Akbar!", that ever welcome note,
So loud and clear and sonorous, comes from the ansar's throat.
"No one but Muslim gives that cry, it is the azan call,
Praise be to God! they are our friends, for they are Muslims all,
What matters it from whence they come, from climate, hot or cold,
From north or south, from east or west, they are in Islam's fold."
So spake Iconia's Sultan, then to Ertoghrul he went,
"Al hamdu li'llah! Praise to God! who thee to us hath sent,
Ask what ye may, brother and friend, I grant it now to thee,
For well I know that Allah hath, this day sent thou to me."
Upon the field that they had won, Iconia's Sultan then,
Did grant the land of Angora, unto those gallant men,
'Twas thus that the Right-hearted man so to Angora came,
The father he of Osman bold, eternal be his fame!
Osmanlis all, where e'er ye be, as long as time remain,
Remember ye, brave Ertoghrul upon Angora's plain,
And rest assured, when in distress, no matter how or where,
Allah will ever hear thy cry and ever heed thy prayer.[3]

---

2   "Bedr's field", the battle of Badr in 2AH/624CE, where the pagan Quraysh of Mecca confronted the Muslims of Medina; the angels came to the aid of the Muslims.

3   Historical Poems, *SHA*, pp.61–4. Depicted as the poem so pleasing to Murad Khan IV when it was brought to his attention that he recalled Sheikh Haroun to court from his exile in Aleppo in 1048H/1639CE (Introduction, *SHA*, p.32).

Moral Poems

AL MIRAJ (THE VISION)

I dream'd a dream, a vision of the night,
I see it still, it stands before my sight;
Methought I stroll'd within a shady wood,
And there, behold, God's Holy Prophet stood,
Clouded his brow, his noble eye was sad,
I wonder'd much, what trouble Ahmed had,
He, Allah's prophet, who so blest as he?
"The chosen one," how could he troubled be?
E'en as I stood, and wonder'd as I stood,
In a stately speech, thus spake the Prophet good:
"Thy thoughts I read, thy mind I know full well,
List to my words, while now to thee I tell
Cause of my woe, and burden of my grief,
Would 'twere not so, 'twould give my mind relief,"
He rais'd his hand, and then to my surprise,
In mirror clear, the earth lay 'fore my eyes;
Monarchs I saw, likewise their subjects too,
Muslim and Pagan, Nazarene and Jew,
Herded together, living cheek by jowl,
Their actions filthy and their language foul;
A king surrounded by a motley crew,
Flatt'rers and pimps, but not a man there true;
Soldiers who fought, not as in days of old,
In honour's cause, but sole for greed of gold.
I saw rich men, with all that wealth could buy,
Heedless of those, who e'en for bread did cry,
I saw, alas, triumphant brazen vice,
And virtue scorn'd. My heart went cold as ice,
At what I saw, for all did seem to tell,
This was not earth, or if earth, earth was hell.
With sorrow'd mind at deeds so done by men,
I clos'd my eyes to hide the sight—and then
The prophet said, "On Mecca's burning sand,
Was it for this, I rais'd aloft the brand,

The torch of truth, and preach'd to all mankind,
A *tarik* plain, salvation sure to find?
Was it for this, I on Mount Hira sat,
And patient was, when kaffeers[1] jeer'd and spat?
Was it for this, that in Mount Hira's cave,
The angel came, and me God's message gave?
Was it for this, the Koran blest was sent?
Is it for naught, I call'd men to repent?
I toil'd, I strove, to led men unto bliss,
With what result? To see a world like this!"
"Prophet of God!" in anguish cried I then,
"What must be done, to save poor wretched men,
To banish vice, to virtue give fresh birth,
To banish hell, and heaven place on earth?
If such can be, I pray reveal the plan,
Which will produce such blessed state for man."
The Prophet smil'd, and then in accents clear,
Spake he these words, "*Kardash*,[2] have no fear.
This world and all can be for ever blest,
If men will learn to value what is best,
And learn to strive, not for themselves alone,
But each for all, and all for ev'ry one,
Then on the earth, aye on this very ground
Peace then shall reign, and Paradise be found,
When in the world, all o'er the land and sea,
Men shall be *men*, and men shall brothers be."[3]

---

1   *Kaffeers* (*kāfirs* or *kāfirūn*), unbelievers.
2   *Kardash*, Brother.
3   Moral Poems, *SHA*, p.67–9; also in Léon, "Life and Poetry of Sheikh Haroun Abdullah", *Asiatic Review*, pp.433–4. Depicted as the poem that led to the exiling of Sheikh Haroun from the Ottoman court to Aleppo, as it "was construed as a reflection upon the reigning Sultan and his courtiers. Its scathing attack bitterly offended the Court...." (Introduction, *SHA*, p.29) This may reflect what Quilliam saw as the ultimate cause of his own "exile" from England (1908–9) to silence his critique of Britain's hardening anti-Ottoman stance.

HER KISHI YEAR (EVERY MAN TO HIS PLACE)

Dervish tekiyeda, hadji mekkeda, tujjar pazarda
(The dervish to the monastery, the pilgrim to Mecca,
the merchant to the bazaar.)

In this world 'tis meet and right that everything should fit,
And so within the *téké* bare, there let the dervish sit,
In *mèdressah*, the scholar and the student are at home,
To Mecca let the hadji go, and Nazar stay at Rome.[1]
The Jew claims no land dear, as that devoted to his birth,
Therefore 'tis meet that he should be, a wand'rer o'er the earth.
The merchant keen on *charsi* and in *pazar* best is found,[2]
The labourer in the fields should be, tilling there the ground,
The sailor in his vessel trim, swift sailing o'er the main,
The soldier on the battle field, fresh laurels there to gain,
Each man to his own fatherland, his faith and to his race,
There's work on earth for each to do, and for each one a place;
So stand ye not in idleness, put courage in your heart,
And having found your work to do, then in it do your part.[3]

---

1   *Téké*, monastery (Sufi lodge); *mèdressah* (madrasa), college; Nazar, contraction of Nazarene
     (Christian).
2   *Charsi*, market; *pazar*, bazaar.
3   Moral Poems, *SHA*, p.70.

MARTRUZGARLARI (MARCH WINDS)

Wa min àyàtihi un yursil-ur-riyaha, mubashiratin wa liyuziqakum
min rahmatihi.
One of the signs of Allah is the sending of the winds, bearing welcome tidings,
that thereby He may cause you to taste of his mercy.
Sura 30, Ar-Rôm (The Greeks), Koran.[1]

'Tis cold, 'tis bleak, the wind and rain
Careering wild o'er mound and plain,
Betoken March is here again,
  All hurly-burly;

Now down the hill, now up the height,
Now blown to left, now blown to right,
Now soaking rain, now tempest quite,
  All surly-whirly.

Yet learn that from those blust'ring hours,
That final grasp of Winter's powers,
April will come, with milder showers,
  To lead on Summer.

And after Nisan,[2] then comes May,
When days grow long, and hearts are gay,
When sweet birds sing, and blythe[3] as they,
  The bee, the hummer.

---

1 As was his habitual practice, Quilliam's partial citation of the Qur'an *Sûrat al-Rûm* 30:46
  is a modified version of George Sale's translation of 1734. He takes out Sale's inclusion of
  the common interpretation of "welcome tidings" as rain in the text, preferring a more literal
  rendering, see Nasr, S.H. et al, *The Study Qur'an* (New York: Harper Collins, 2015), p.995.
  Quilliam/Léon glosses the name of the chapter *al-Rûm* as "Greeks" rather than the more
  prevalent rending of "Byzantines" or "Romans", presumably referring to the use of Greek as the
  administrative language of the Byzantines mentioned in 30:2, after which the chapter takes its
  name.
2 Nisan, April.
3 Blythe, alternative spelling of blithe, *OED* 1st Edn.

And after Mayis[4] cometh June,
And none can say it comes too soon,
And sun is bright, while hearts keep tune,
    And grow the lighter;

July succeeds, and in its season,
The harvest comes; now let us reason,
And think it out, sans jest or treason,
    And be the brighter.

In life at times, do we not find,
Dark days indeed, with blust'ring wind,
And treatment hard, and words unkind,
    That seem to freeze us?

But gentler words and brighter day,
Do come and drive the clouds away,
And prove to us, the darksome day
    Was sent to tease us.

Bear all your ills with steady heart;
E'er do your best, act well your part,
And thro' the clouds, be sure, will dart
    A sunbeam glancing.

When brighter days do come at last,
And sun disperse the sky o'ercast,
You then will find the troubles past,
    Your joys enhancing.[5]

---

4   Mayis, May.
5   Moral Poems, *SHA*, pp.71–3.

IKI HADJI (THE TWO TRAVELLERS)

Two travellers went out one day,
  And walk'd a piece together,
One found that flow'rlets strew'd his way
  And pleasant was the weather.

Balmy the air, the sky all blue,
  And sweet bloomed the flowers;
"Praise God," he said, "for all I view,
  Sweet is this world of ours."

Where'er he went, he felt content,
  And smil'd on each wayfarer;
His smile a gleam of sunshine sent,
  No sunbeam could be fairer.

To each he'd say, a blythe "Good day,
  And brighter still good morrow";
His words, as sweet as skylark's lay,
  Seem'd made to soften sorrow.

And when of life, he was bereft,
  And found e'en higher pleasure,
In world beyond; the world he'd left,
  His mem'ry sweet did treasure.

Within a turbah's[1] hallow'd walls,
  His body rests in slumber,
His soul hath sped, at angels' call,
  'Mongst saints he's joined the number.

The other traveller thro' life,
  As long the road he trudgèd
Seem'd ever to engage in strife,
  A kind word e'en he grudgèd.

---

1 Turbah (turbe), tomb.

For him no sun shone bright and gay,
        For him no flow'rlets bloomèd:
Dark e'er the sky, and dull the day,
        And happiness was doomèd.

On all he met, he'd glare and scowl,
        The bees e'en ceased from humming,
The children ran, the dogs did howl,
        Whene'er they saw him coming.

And when he died, then no one sigh'd,
        And some said "'Tis a pity,
That years ago, this did betide,
        'Twere better for the city."

His grave lies there, a mound quite bare,
        And weeds do it encumber;
No one doth care, if dogs lie there,
        They leave them there to slumber.

For your own sake, a lesson take,
        From what I've just been rhyming;
It rests, my friend, with you to make
        Harsh sounds, or pleasant chiming.

A cheerful heart, will bliss impart,
        And often eases sorrow;
So start at once, and do *your* part,
        And don't wait till to-morrow.

And learn this lesson, learn it well,
        'Tis by your own endeavour,
This earth is made a heav'n or hell;
        This rule holds good for ever.[2]

---

2   Moral Poems, *SHA*, pp.74–6.

MAYDAN (THE RACE OF LIFE)

At ölör, maydani qalur; qahriman ölör shani qalur.
(The horse dies, the racecourse remains; the hero dies, his fame endures.)

Within the heart's most inmost cell, a voice calls to thee, man,
This be the message that it tell, "Thy life is but a span,
From whence thou came, thou knowest not; nor dost thou ever know,
What is on earth to be thy lot, nor where to go, thou wilt go;
And yet in one thing find support, and on it rest, O man!
Thou'rt not created thus for sport, but by determin'd plan,
A part thou art of one vast whole, eternal and unbound,
A spark, thou, of that blazing coal, that lightens all around;
Whilst here thou dwellest on the earth thro' ev'ry passing year,
From e'en the moment of thy birth, do thou, thy work, sincere,
Run thou thy race, the prize to gain, e'er strive to do thy best,
And steadfast to the end remain, to Allah leave the rest;
And if thou die upon the road, ere thou hast seen thy gains,
The race-horse dies, but where it stood, the racecourse still remains;
The hero of a thousand fields, has but a task as yours,
And when 'tis done, his spirit yields, but still his fame endures;
Fresh courage take then to thy heart, and never be downcast,
God knowest those who do their part, and will reward at last."[1]

---

1   Moral Poems, *SHA*, pp.77–8.

MUHIMM JUZÍ-SHÈY
(THE IMPORTANCE OF LITTLE THINGS)

There was a man, a Mussulman, and Youssuff was his name,
Who wanted noble to become, and all to know his fame;
And so each day to mosque he went and fervent there he pray'd,
That *rakats*[1] twelve each pray'r he made, such fervour he displayed,
His zeal so great to make his pray'r, so great indeed the stake,
That ev'ry day he quite forgot his *abdest* first to make,
And so each day, *jenabat* he, within the mosque did sit,
Forgetting that when *teniz dey'l*, to pray he was not fit;[2]
For full twelve months he pray'd and pray'd, but ne'er an answer got,
"*Vway Bashima!*" he groaned and said "*bedbatchliq* is my lot."[3]
Then while he sadly groaned and moan'd, and madly beat his head,
Behold an angel 'fore him stood, and sternly to him said:
"*Budala* knowest not full well that which the law declares,
That he would Allah approach, *temiz* must come to prayers?"
"Yes *Meleka*," Youssuff replied, "that I have understood;[4]
But that was such a trifling thing, I deem'd it of no good."
"*Ahmaq!*"[5] the angry angel said, in accents stern and cold,
"Pray, who art thou to disregard a command clear and old?
Learn thou, O fool, this lesson well, and take it keen to heart,
It is of grains the rock is made, tho' small may be each part;
If thou to greatness would attain, each moment and each hour,
Nought must be thought too little, for each thing has a power,
It is by inches we advance, just one step at a time,
He who would reach the mountain top, persistently must climb,
To those who small things faithful do, with conscience true and clear,
Allah will give success on earth and their petitions hear,
If thou would'st then success attain, the small things ne'er despise,
Neglect them not and ever strive, and thine shall be the prize."[6]

---

1   *Rakat*, literally "a bending", the division into which Muslim prayers are made.
2   *Abdest*, ablution; *jenabat*, unclean; *teniz dey'l*, unclean.
3   *Vway bashima!*, Ill luck is on my head!; *bedbatchliq*, misfortune.
4   *Budala*, foolish one; *temiz*, clean; *meleka*, angel.
5   *Ahmaq*, fool.
6   Moral Poems, *SHA*, pp.79–80.

MEDH PEYGHAMBERIN
(A GHAZAL IN PRAISE OF THE PROPHET)

So long as the heart doth pulsate and beat,
So long as the sun bestows light and heat,
So long as the blood thro' our veins doth flow,
So long as the mind in knowledge doth grow,
So long as the tongue retains power of speech,
So long as wise men true wisdom do teach,
The praise of God's Prophet, Ahmed the Blest,
Shall flow from our lips and spring from our breast,
'Twas Rasul-Allah from darkness of night
Did lead us to Truth, did give to us light,
Did point out the path, which follow'd with zest,
Leadeth to Islam and gives Peace and Rest.
Praise be to Allah! 'Twas He who did send,
Ahmed Muhammad, our Prophet, our Friend.[1]

---

1   Moral Poems, *SHA*, p.81. Included in this collection of Sheikh Haroun's poetry, it was originally published as "A Ghazel by Prof. Haroun Mustapha Léon, M.A., Ph.D., F.S.P." in "In Praise of the Prophet", *IR* (Woking), June 1915, p.286.

TAZÍR (THE REBUKE)

Mal insanilè ilsan olmaz,
Fakirlik aib deil, tenbellik aib dir.
Wealth does not make the man;
Poverty is no sin, but laziness is.

It chanc'd one day, there hap'd to stray along a country road,
To take *hawà*[,] *fadul* Najà, far from his own abode;
High in the sky, *ghùnèsh*, bright eye, so flaming fierce did shine,[1]
So great the heat, upon him beat, to rest he did incline,
So on the ground, 'neath tree he found, he lay him down at ease,
Enjoy'd the shade, as there he laid, such shelter did him please.
In *tarla* by, there caught his eye, busy upon the soil,
A *renjbèr poor,* a country boer, with diligence did toil;
His *kàmiss* torn, his *shalwar* worn, his *pàpuch* old and soil'd,[2]
'Twas plain to see, that poverty, was lot of him that toil'd.
"You fellow there, *fakir rènjbèr,*"[3] did loudly Najà bawl,
"Come here I say, Come now this way, Come quickly to my call."
With humble mien, Ala-ud-deen (such was the *rènjbèr's* name),
Laid down his hoe, and straight did go, t'wards place whence call had came.
"*Effendim*[4] say, what woulds't to-day, thou of me now demand?
This very hour, if in my power, it is at thy command;
I've apples three, here now with me, they're thine if thou desire,
I've bread and cheese, partake of these, if thou dost them require.
A pitcher too, refreshing *su*,[5] I'll bring from river brink,
'Tis bright and clear, and flows quite near, refreshing 'tis to drink."

---

1   *Hawà fadul* Najà, the fresh air, wealthy Proud (used as a name here); *ghùnèsh*, the Sun.
2   *Tarla*, a cultivated or ploughed field; *renjbèr*, peasant; *kàmiss*, shirt; *shalwar*, trousers; *pàpuch*, boots.
3   *Fakir rènjbèr*, poor peasant.
4   *Effendim*, my lord.
5   *Su*, water.

"*Deli eshek! Bosh lakirdjek!*[6] What folly dost thou tell?
Thinkst of thy meat, that I would eat, or drink from out thy well?
Thou silly ass, as green as grass, whatever be thy name,
Thou *parasiz*, thou *akilsiz*, hast thou in thee no shame,[7]
With *kàmiss* torn, and *shalwàr* worn, to stand before me now?
Thy poverty should bring to thee, a blush upon thy brow."
Raising his head, the *rènjbèr* said:—"I'm poor I know full well,
That is no ill, 'Tis Allah's will, His reason none can tell,
No crime in me, is poverty, I do all that I can,
Not *zenghanlik*, makes *merdanlik*, 'tis not the wealth makes man.[8]
I work, with heart, to do my part, no lazy man am I,
No sin or shame, is on my name, or doth upon me lie;
Shèrm is on he, who lazy be, *tenbellik jùnhà dir*,
Of we twain here, which most to fear, Allah's *darghinlik*,[9] sir?"[10]

---

6   *Deli eshek! Bosh lakirdjek!*, Mad ass! Empty, foolish talk!
7   *Parasiz*, pauper; *akilsiz*, senseless.
8   *Zeghanlik*, riches or wealth; *merdanlik*, manliness.
9   *Shèrm*, shame; *tenbellik jùnhà dir*, laziness is a sin; *darghinlik*, displeasure.
10 Moral Poems, *SHA*, pp.82–4.

Miscellaneous Poems

SABAH YAZI (A SUMMER MORNING)

The sunshine gaily smiling, cerulean blue the sky,
The flowers lovely petals, on which the dewdrops lie;
Those shining little dewdrops, that flash there in the sun
Like coronet of diamonds, heralding day begun.
The skylark singing sweetly, to welcome thus the day;
The perfume of the meadows, all redolent with hay.
From out the ground is springing, the swiftly growing corn;
All nature joyous, happy; it is a summer's morn!
Come let us join the chorus, that birds and flow'rlets sing,
And chant, with joyous nature, a hymn to nature's King.[1]

---

1   Miscellaneous Poems, *SHA*, p.87.

KEREMLIQ (KINDLINESS)

The richest gem that e'er adorn'd the greatest monarch's brow;
Most fertile field to harvest yield whenever turn'd by plough;
The sweetest perfume e'er distill'd, from leaf of fragrant rose;
The choicest incense ever burnt, or balm for human woes;
The dulcet strain of harmony, or cooing of the dove;
The sweetest thrill of rapture from the tender chord of love;
The song and chant that angels bright in rapture ever breathe;
A chaplet of ne'er fading flow'rs, all tender hearts may wreathe;
The brightest star bedecks the sky, with never failing light;
The guerdon which doth never fail those who do strive for right;
The choicest wine that ever came from *azum* when 'twas prest;[1]
Is kindliness, so sweet and pure, within the human breast.[2]

---

1   *Guerdon*, reward or requital (from Old French, poetic and rhetorical, *OED* 1st Edn.); *azum*, grapes.
2   Miscellaneous Poems, *SHA*, p.88.

SEV HEPSI SEV (LOVE, ALWAYS LOVE)

So staid, so calm, so just, 'twas thus that Reason stood,
Inviting all to come and listen for their good.
"Be ever ruled by me; be guided by my plan,
And happiness secure, will be thy lot, oh man!
Trust not a handsome face; beware of woman's smile,
Their sex deceitful is and ever doth beguile;
But ever virtue prize, and look with it for health,
What matter if be plain the maid who haveth wealth?
'Mongst such find thou thy mate; possessing such a wife,
Then shalt thou, Reason saith, enjoy a happy life."
"Excuse me, dame," said one, "for I am dire perplex'd,
Thou'st left one item out, tho' 'tis a question vex'd,
And in this matter grave, must bear a mighty part,
Thou'st reckoned of the head, but now what of the heart?"
"That portion of thy frame," then slowly Reason said,
"Will lead thee far astray, 'cept governed by thy head,
If thou art ruled by me, and prove thyself thus wise,
The head thou wilt regard, the heart thou wilt despise,
Such fancies lay aside, let reason be thy rule,
He that doth disobey, doth prove himself a fool."
"Such, Reason, thou may think, such, Reason, thou may preach,
Yet 'tis in vain thou cry, in vain such doctrine teach,
Men ever will be men, and to the end of time,
So long as women be, and long as poets rhyme,
They'll make one thing their theme, they'll make one end their goal.
And to attain this end will risk immortal soul,
Throw Reason to the winds, and ever, always prove,
That strongest power e'er be, the mighty power of Love."[1]

---

1   Miscellaneous Poems, *SHA*, pp.89–90.

NASSIHAT (ADVICE)

If thou wouldst fight curs'd Shaitan[1] well, and all his trusty imps,
Gamesters, usurers, courtesans, and all their filthy pimps,
Stand fast to Faith, perform thy work, and to thyself be true,
And leave to curs and wastrels, thou, the devil and his crew.[2]

---

1   Shaitan, Satan, the Prince of Evil.
2   Miscellaneous Poems, *SHA*, pp.91.

BIQHUDLUQ (ECSTASY)

Oh! learned men and wise, give ear unto my strain,
And I will thee apprise how peace thou canst attain,
Thy knowledge and thy skill, alone, is all in vain,
Only by Allah's will canst thou perfection gain;
Thou canst not buy with gold, nor rubies of the best
That which is never sold, north, south, nor east, nor west;
In caves for it ne'er seek, nor on the mountain crest,
Within thy heart, when meek, there make thy patient quest;
'Tis not the proud of heart that Allah wise doth choose,
But he who doth his part and ever Allah woos,
Who chants the sacred name and doth upon it muse,
Who, paradise to gain, his very self doth lose;
To such doth Allah come, and doth with him abide,
His vices doth benumb, and dwelleth by his side,
Close as the vein to heart, yet as creation wide,
Mercy and love impart, whatever may betide.
To me of gold ne'er talk, of rubies never sing,
To you I will not hark of any earthly thing;
My *kulah* I prefer to crown of any king,
My *zikr* and my pray'r doth peace unto me bring;
From Salsabil I drink, 'tis sweeter far than wine,[1]
For me do sweet birds sing, for me the sun doth shine,
For me doth Cafur flow, and Zenjebil is mine,[2]
For Allah is in me, and, Allah, I am thine.[3]

---

1   *Kulah*, the Dervish cap; *zikr*, a form of worship (remembrance of Allah); Salsabil, one of the fountains of Paradise.
2   Cafur (*Kāfūr*) and Zenjebil (*Zanjabīl*); Quilliam notes that these are names of fountains in Paradise. However, *kāfūr* can also mean camphor, while *zanjabīl* means ginger, both of which are mixed with paradisal spring water as a drink.
3   Miscellaneous Poems, *SHA*, pp.92–3.

PART 3

Translations
(1927–31)

IN PRAISE OF ABDUL-LATĪF AL-BAGHDADI

Translated from As-Sa'id ibn-Sūrat al-Mulk, the poet and qadi, in praise of the Arab physician and theologian, Abdul-Latīf al-Baghdadi.

The art of Galen only doth the body heal,
But Ibn Imran's art body and soul doth feel.
His wisdom great, sickness of ignorance so dire,
Sure could he heal and cause it to expire.
If moon submits itself unto his art,
Her blots and spots he will cause to depart,
Her periodic effects, I am sure,
His art and skill would very quickly cure.
Her full moon face would shine perfectly clear,
And thus remain throughout the changing year,
And in her time of conjunction painting,
Abu Imran's[1] skill, would save her waning.[2]

---

1 Abu 'Imran Musa ibn Maymun ibn 'Ubayd Allah was the Arabic name by which the renowned Jewish philosopher, rabbinical authority and practising physician, Maimonides (1138–1204CE), was known.
2 Haroun Mustapha Léon, "Medicine and Psychology under the Khalifs I", *IC*, 1927, Vol.1, No.3, pp.388–406 (pp.399–400).

UNTITLED (1928A)

A little spark will soon ignite if fann'd into a flame,
A little thing will cause a war. How dreadful is the same?
But if it's nurs'd with care and skill, how useful is a fire?
And Judam know how war to wage, and thus gain their desire.
A little seed will impregnate the *ma'z*[1] with hairs like silk,
And in due time, the kid appears, then you the goat can milk,
So 'tis with war, when wag'd with care, yet e'er with might and main,
And careful art, the battle's smart will bring its victors gain.[2]

---

1   *Ma'z*, a goat.
2   Haroun Mustapha Léon, "Ibnu'l Kirriya, The Desert Orator", *IC*, 1928, Vol.2, No.3, pp.347–59
    (p.352). Ibnu'l-Kirriya to Hajjaj, based on Slane, Vol.I, pp.236–43.

UNTITLED (1928B)

Wajib ul takrim[1] there should always be three,
The *alim*, the *hakim*, and thy *muhib* they be.[2]
To slight the learned is 'gainst Islamic rule,
And proves that the slighter is naught but a fool;
Slight not the *hakim* or you'll learn, p'raps too late
That, for your folly, you have lost your estate;
As for your friend, you will find, soon indeed,
That the true *muhib* stands by you, when in need.[3]

---

1 *Wajib ul takrim*, held in honour.
2 *Alim*, learned; *hakim*, magistrate; *muhib*, friend.
3 *DJA*, 7th April 1928, p.3, versified form of a saying attributed to Ibn Abi Duwad, see H.M.
   Léon, "Ancient Arabian Poets III", *IC*, 1929, Vol.3, No.3, p.406.

ZU'N NÛN AL-MISRI

For Thee, Belov'd One, art e'er in my heart
For my love of Thee can never depart.
All blame on me cast, I scorn and despise;
Thou art to me all, whate'er may arise.
For Thy sake, belov'd, I yield up my all,
Content as victim for Thy sake to fall.
To love and to serve Thee, 'tis all I ask,
Endure Thy absence, impossible task![1]

1   Haroun Mustapha Léon, "Ancient Arabian Poets: a Muslim saint and poet of the third century of the hijrah. Zu'n Nûn al-Misri", *IC*, 1929, Vol.3, No.1; pp.56–74 (p.68); *DJA*, 11th February 1928, p.8. Léon's poem is inspired by a prose translation in Slane, Vol.I, p.292.

THE QASIDA
(OR ELEGY) OF THE GRANDSON OF IBN AL-TAAWIZI

May, a spring-tide shower, gentle and bright,
As honey'd-dew, descend on thee by night;
When the morn arise, may no evil eye,
With pestilent spell glance up at the sky,
The beneficent clouds to charm away,
That sweetly descent on thee in the day.
The willow of the sand, that is unique and rare
Grown on ground reserved and e'er tended with care,
The fair maiden, whose form is pliant and slender,
Whose soul is e'er pure and whose heart ever tender;
Such once my ambition and my heart's full desire,
With consuming passion and my soul all afire.
But alas for the change! for nought charms me now,
What care I for the sand or the tree's swaying bough?
The house is quite empty, and the bird from there flown,
My eyes they are weeping and I only can groan;
My friend has departed, such, alas! is my fate,
My desire unfulfilled, and my heart desolate.
A house without inmate, that can ne'er be a home;
Is the depth of the sea never more than the foam?
It was friends and their thoughts that made the home alive,
When departed the bees silent then is the hive!
The stones do not speak, they are silent and dead
Silent is the palace, when the monarch has fled.
In days that are past, in the years now gone by
The fair moon and the stars bejewelled the sky,
In gardens were roses, and who could then tell,
On mountains, the number there were of gazelle?
My mind was then dazzled, for such beauty was there;
Now alas! all is dark and my mind in despair.
Like silver the moon then shone so brightly above,
And a maiden, nymph-like, had encaptured my love;
I remember the night, I can recall it well,
With what frantic delight, how my bosom did swell
When the one that I lov'd, she the pearl I did prize
With her well-moulded arm, and her lustrous dark eyes,

Me handed the goblet, to the brim fill'd with wine;
Like her cheek it was blushing, and all seem'd divine.
'Drink now,' she then bade me, 'that good health we enjoy,
With long life to us both, to our love no alloy!'
As loose as her garments seem'd her soul free of care;
Her ankles encircled with such choice jewels rare,
In a setting of gold, in a well-fashion'd ring,
Was it she, or the gold the most precious thing?
With love my heart teem'd. Alas! hers was a void
With my heart she but play'd, with my love she but toy'd;
A mere glance at her lips fervent love did inspire,
And her languished glance at once fann'd my desire;
If with rich youthful slap her fair veins are all fill'd,
All her mind and her body still pure and unstill'd,
From her lips how I long yet, with ecstatic bliss,
Sweetest nectar to draw in one long, loving kiss.
Her bright eyes and a sword to each other are kin,
Each possesses a scabbard made of purest skin;
When the eyelids are clos'd then the eye underneath
Is hidden and harmless like the sword in its sheath;
But when eyes are glancing and lancing in the day,
No sword hath the power so to conquer and slay.
It is for this reason, that, in the tongue of man,
The scabbard for the sword is called "*al-ajfan*".[1]

---

1   *Al-ajfan*; the eyelids, plural of *jafn*, eyelid. Léon, "Ancient Arabian Poets", *IC*, 1929, Vol.3, No.1, pp.71–2; *DJA*, 18th February 1928, p.2; *SAP*, pp.16–17. Léon's poetic rendition, cf. the prose translation in Slane, Vol.I, p.293.

TRIBUTE TO ZU'N NÛN AL-MISRI

Beneath that dome, in hallow'd ground,
Sheykh Zu'n-Nûn rests, his friends around.
I said they rest—I mean their clay
Lies there until Judgement Day.[1]

---

1   Léon, "Ancient Arabian Poets", *IC*, 1929, Vol.3, No.1, p.74; *SAP*, p.14. his poetic rendition, cf.
    Slane, Vol.I, p.293:"A chapel has been built over his tomb, and in this chapel are the graves of a
    number of other holy men...." Léon corrects "chapel" with "dome".

A dragon is a dreadful beast, as all of us can tell,
On men and maidens he will feast, and animals as well;
But when At-Tinnîn plays his lute and music sweet does make,
The *Tays* and *Mu'zat*,[1] sure of foot, attention prompt do take.
From plain and hill, from mount and crag, they speed from all around,
And quick of foot and all agog, list to the music's sound.
Sure, ne'er was dragon so expert, sure ne'er was beast so cute,
As At-Tinnîn, who doth not hurt, but charms goats with his lute.[2]

---

1   "He-goat" and "she-goats" respectively.
2   Haroun Mustapha Léon, "Ancient Arabian Poets II: the poet prince who became a Khalifah", *IC*, 1929, Vol.3, No.2, pp.249–72 (p.250); *DJA*, 25th February 1928, p.2; *SAP*, p.25. Likely a poetic inspiration based on Ibn Khallikan's biographical note on Ibrahim al-Mahdi (see Slane, Vol.I: p.17), half-brother to Harun al-Rashid, whom Léon likens to the Pied Piper of Hamlyn. There does not appear to have been a ninth-century Abbasid poet named Ali ibn Yusuf who wrote courtly panegyrics. There is an Abbasid prince and poet, Yusuf ibn Yusuf ibn Ali ibn Yusuf ibn Ahmad, whose patron was the penultimate Abbasid caliph, al-Mustansir Bi'llah (r. 1226–42), see S. Al-Safadi, *Al-Wafi bi al-Wafayat* (Beirut: Dar Ihya' al-Turath al-'Arabi, 2000), 29 vols, Vol.16, p.167.

THE ASSASSINATION OF AL-MA'MUN'S VIZIER

Ill-omened, said, that morning, then, the star show'd in the skies,
Water and fire mix not, Fadl, therein the danger lies.
For, when they mix, that is the time that thou hast cause to dread,
For in that hour, in cruel way, then shall thy blood be shed.

In calm content, to bathe he went, and thought he'd nought to fear;
"My blood is shed, the water's red, the course is now quite clear."
So said Fadl, no thought of ill in his mind did abide;
The stars imply that which is nigh, Fate cannot be denied!
For as he came forth from the same, four ruffians, dark and grim.
The signal gave, like angry wave, they threw themselves on him
Their daggers flash, his flesh they gash, their knives they stain with gore,
Three minutes sped, and he was dead, proud Fadl was no more.[1]

---

1   Léon, "Ancient Arabian Poets II", *IC*, 1929, Vol.3, No.2, pp.259–60; *DJA*, 10th March 1928, p.2; cf. Slane, Vol.II, pp.474–5. *SAP*, pp.35–6. The assassination of Al-Ma'mun's vizier, an expert astrologer who thought to ward off an ill-omen that his blood would be shed between fire and water, having himself bled beforehand in a hot bath he thought he evaded any ill-fate. Another poetic inspiration of Léon's that is misattributed to "Ali ibn Yusuf".

UNTITLED (1929B)

Who has not heard of dragons fierce and strange, of wondrous make,
With pow'rful jaws like crocodile, and tails like those of snake,
While fire and smoke from nostrils come to foul the air around.
Sure, such a grim and awful beast can never else be found,
Their appetite, though wondrous great, yet is so strict and nice,
Of maidens fair, just one a day, and nought else will suffice.
But now I learn a wondrous thing, a dragon dress'd in clothes.
From his late den hath fled away, and as a woman goes,
Sure, ne'er was this e'er heard before, throughout the world's long age,
A dragon flies with trembling knees, and wars no longer rage.[1]

1   Léon, "Ancient Arabian Poets II", *IC*, 1929, Vol.3, No.2, pp.262–3; *DJA*, 17th March 1928, p.2; *SAP*, p.39. Attributed to an anonymous court poet writing on the flight of Ibrahim ibn Mahdi from Baghdad in 204AH/818CE "disguised as a negress slave". It could be one of Léon's compositions.

UNTITLED (1929C)

Maidens there be whose skin is dark, aye e'en as black as ink,
In conduct spotless yet they be, and from all evil shrink,
So clear and pure their conscience is that of them e'en the sight
Causes *kâfûr*[1] to earnest wish that it was black, not white,
'Why am not I sweet smelling musk, this maid to emulate?'
So sighs *kâfûr* in whispers low, not content with its fate.
Regard the eye, look at it well, its *bubbu*[2] may look dark.
Yet merely it doth concentrate the light within its ark,
And seeming dark, yet is the light, 'tis to the eye the heart
O man, then know, that, in the eye, 'tis the important part.[3]

---

1 *kâfûr*, camphor. In Arabian poetry camphor is often used as a symbol of whiteness, and musk as emblematic of black.
2 *bubbu*, the pupil of the eye.
3 Léon, "Ancient Arabian Poets II", *IC*, 1929, Vol.3, No.2, pp.265–6; *DJA*, 17th March 1928, p.2; *SAP*, pp.41–2. A poetic reworking of the Baron's prose translation of a nineteenth-century Arab poet, Ibn Kalakis, see Slane, Vol.I, p.18: "There are females dark in skin, but in conduct clear and pure; whose presence would induce the (white) camphor to envy the (black) musk: 'tis thus with the pupil of the eye; men think it black, though merely (concentrated) light."

UNTITLED (1929D)

A maid possess'd of ev'ry charm that youth and beauty give,
Well poised head, well rounded arm, and eyes that look and live;
For her my muse I do attune, for her I look and long,
My passion hot as sun at noon, and fever'd is my song,
Her ruby lips I fain would press, and taste the nectar there;
Oh, how can I in words express the love I feel for her?
Here, in my heart, doth anguish grow, companion with my joy,
One glance from her makes passion grow and doth my peace destroy.
O lovely maid! Return my love, which you alone inspire,
Come to my arms, a trembling dove; grant me all I desire!
Oh, give this panting bosom ease—I can love none but thee;
Oh, say my song thy soul doth please, and thou'lt belong to me![1]

1   Léon, "Ancient Arabian Poets II", *IC*, 1929, Vol.3, No.2, pp.270–1; *DJA*, 24th March 1928, p.2;
    SAP, p.47. A translation from the famous Abbasid court poet, Abu Nuwas, about whom see
    Slane, Vol.I, pp.391–5.

UNTITLED (1929E)

Behold a mystery I'll tell, a thing surprising rare,
So come with me to Sarr-man-rai, and see what's lying there.
In narrow space and close confin'd, within a chamber dark,
There doth repose in quietude a man who made his mark,
Who, in his time play'd many parts—I think, at least a score.
Them to relate, much time would take a month or even more.
A prince, a king, a dragon brave, a singer of sweet lay,
A fisherman, a negress slave, a player on the *nay*.[1]
One who could charm upon the lute the am'rous horned goat,
And also soothe a king to sleep with music sweet to note.
You doubt my word, you scorn my muse, as a mere passing whim,
But all is true, if thou wilt view, the tomb of Ibrâhîm.[2]

---

1   *Nay*, flute.
2   Léon, "Ancient Arabian Poets II", *IC*, 1929, Vol.3, No.2, p.272; *DJA*, 24th March 1928, p.2;
    SAP, p.48. Said to be a translation of the lesser-known Ali Yunus or possibly Abu Nuwas,
    written after the death and burial of Ibrahim al-Mahdi, but likely to be another one of Léon's
    compositions.

AL-'ALAMAT WA'L-ISHARAT (SIGNS AND WONDERS)

There are signs to people of understanding.
Qur'ân, Sûrah II. Al-Baqarah ("The Cow").[1]

On Nature's self there hangs the very breath of God,
The fragrance of the flowers, the dew upon the sod;
The birds, in melody, their dulcet voices raise,
And all creation joins to celebrate His praise;
The zephyr gently glides thro' vales amid the hills,
And sweetly adds its song to those of rippling rills,
And when, at eve is spent the ever fleeting day
The earth is silver limn'd beneath the moon's soft ray.
At such a time I mused, and thus my musing ran:
"Give thanks to Allah for his gifts to thee, oh man."[2]

---

1   Sale, 2:164 (partial), p.23.
2   Haroun Mustapha Léon, "Ancient Arabian Poets III: Ibn Abi Duwad The Humane Qadi",
     IC, 1929, Vol.3, No.3, pp.404–26 (p.405); *DJA*, 7th April 1928, p.3. Léon credits the poem's
     ascription by Abu'l-'A'ina to Ahmad ibn Abi Duwad (776–854), a poet and judge, close friend of
     Al-Ma'mun and chief judge under Al-Mu'tasim, during which time he led the famous state trial
     against Ahmad ibn Hanbal. A committed Mu'tazilite, Ibn Abi Duwad is generally recognized for
     his learning and magnanimity even by his Sunni critics, despite his central role in the Inquisition
     (Mihna), see "Aḥmad b. Abī Du'ād", *EI2*, http://dx.doi.org/10.1163/1573-3912_islam_
     SIM_0391, accessed 1 July 2021.

UNTITLED (1929F)

I love thee in the morning, but I love thee more at night,
When the world is hush'd in silence, and the stars are shining bright;
When the shades of night envelop, then thou art e'er my theme.
My thoughts on thee when waking and thy sweet form when I dream
And when Al-Fajar opens and the birds begin to sing,
And nature's face is radiant in the early blushing spring,
And such blissful joy and gladness there all around to see,
I long for that joy and gladness to share for aye with thee.[1]

---

1 Léon, "Ancient Arabian Poets III", *IC*, 1929, Vol.3, No.3, p.406; *DJA*, 7th April 1928, p.3.
   Ascribed to Ibn Abi Duwad by Di'bil 'Ali al-Khuza'i (765–860CE), a "celebrated poet" famous
   for his satire.

UNTITLED (1929G)

There was rust on the locks and fetters,
And mould and blight on the walls;
There was silence there in the dungeon,
And darkness still in the halls.
A body lay on the mattress,
They, whispering said, "he is dead,"
Al-Buwaiti's form was there lying.
His soul to *Firdaws*[1] had fled.[2]

1   Correction of *Fardus*; *Firdaws*: Paradise.
2   Léon, "Ancient Arabian Poets III", *IC*, 1929, Vol.3, No.3, p.420: The subject of the poem is
     Abu Ya'qub Yusuf al-Buwayti (d.846CE), a student of Imam al-Shafi'i, who was caught up in the
     Mihna (Inquisition) and taken as prisoner to Baghdad, when he refused to accept the createdness
     of the book of the Holy Qur'an, and later died chained up in prison, see Slane, Vol.IV, pp.394–7.
     The poem is unattributed, so presumably it is one of Léon's.

UNTITLED (1929H)

He takes the advantage, when me he sees,
To cease from sitting or bending of knees,
And forthwith stands up and then makes his pray'rs
And this doth because, 'gainst me, hate he bears;
From time he sees me, so long as it lasts,
Pious duties fulfils and keeps the fasts.
May such hatred from him never depart,
But ever stay to envenom his heart;
So fierce may it be that ne'er may it close
That standing or standing (*sic*) give no repose;
That sleep from his eyes, hence ever may flee,
His soul be consum'd, with hatred of me![1]

---

1   Léon, "Ancient Arabian Poets III", *IC*, 1929, 3/3, p.425; claimed to be a translation from the
    vizier under Al-Mu'tasim, Muhammad b. Abd al-Malik Ibn al-Zayyat, speaking of his rival Ibn
    Abu Duwad, see "Ibn al-Zayyāt", *EI2*, http://dx.doi.org/10.1163/1573-3912_islam_SIM_3423,
    accessed 1 July 2021.

UNTITLED (1930A)

O thou, who vainly thinkest to satirize,
Thou exposest thyself to death in so attacking me,
My honour cannot be diminished by the mention of oil,
The reputation of my family is too well established and known,
'Tis you who have *malkuk* [stained] the state with your filthy *qir* [pitch]
Nothing could cleanse the state from the *buqa* (stain)
Until we washed it with our *zayt* (oil)![1]

---

1   Henri Mustapha Léon, "Ancient Arabian Poets III, continued: Ibn Abi Duwad, the humane
     Qadi", *IC*, 1930, Vol.4, No.2, pp.274–90 (p.274); cf, Slane, I, p.69. Ibn Abi Duwad hearing of
     a seventy-line satire against the vizier Ibn al-Zayyat replied with a single verse of his own: "How
     much the state requires a shower of/rain, to wash away that filthy stain of oil", referencing the
     vizier's name, Ibn al-Zayyat (son of the oil-man), see Slane, Vol.III, p.252. The translation by
     Léon is of Ibn al-Zayyat's rejoinder.

UNTITLED (1930B)

Today is blank and dreary, the support of the state has gone,
For his is dead, and we are left, supportless, sad, alone.
He, when he spoke, rich words of pearl, did, dew-like, drop from mouth.
Whose accents were as fragrant e'er as zephyrs from the South.
And his is dead, whose succour was never asked in vain,
Our protector in misfortune, and our comforter in pain.
Today, the path of learning drear, dark, cold and chill as night,
Alas! the sun of generosity, to-day, no more, gives light.
Our hearts are fill'd with sorrow, with tears our eyes o'erflow.
The mist from his last winding sheet, doth dark and darker grow.
Alas that we should see the day, whereon these words are said,
The mighty one has fallen now, our dearest friend is dead.[1]

---

1   Léon, "Ancient Arabian Poets III, continued", *IC*, 1930, Vol.4, No.2, p.284, an unattributed eulogy said at the funeral procession of Ibn Abi Duwad by the first of three poets, cf. Slane, Vol.I, p.71.

RAY SAKIB (GOOD ADVICE)

If you would have your daughter fair,
Then rear her from her 'teens with care;
If on her cheeks bloom rosy pink,
Then give her *halib*[1] pure to drink;
To make her form full plump and nice,
Farraj pilau,[2] of best of rice;
And glossy hair, in tresses long
And dulcet voice, that trills in song
With cheerful mind and heart e'er gay,
Comes to the maid, who bathes each day,
For such an one, need have no care,
She'll find a *husband* anywhere.[3]

---

1 *Halib*, milk.
2 *Farraj pilau*, chicken pilau.
3 Haroun Mustapha Léon, "Ibn At-Tathriyya—The Poet of the Dairy, Part I", *IC*, 1930, Vol.4, No.4, pp.574–87 (p.581). Attributed to Yazid ibn al-Tathriyya (whose nickname was Muwaddik, "the Exciter"), who was so handsome that his very presence excited women, as quoted by the poet Abu Tamman al-Ta'i.

UNTITLED (1930C)

'Tis of the Okalid maid I think and dream,
Envelop'd in robes that like a sandhill seem,
In shape and smoothness, in colour like the sand,
Her waist as slender as the willow wand.
Within the tribal bounds the summer she doth spend
And, after *zuhri*, then her fleeting footsteps bend,
To Na'mân, in the Arak vale soft there to sleep,
While hosts of friendly Jinn do faithful angels keep,
One look at her, though but a timid glance,
Doth me transfix, my soul complete entrance,
My brain doth set on fire, the flames mount high,
A single glance can ne'er me satisfy.
Yet, but one glance from her, however slight,
Doth ravish soul, and fill me with delight.
O idol of my heart! my inmost soul!
To gain thy love is my desire, my goal;
I have no thought, no love, but thee alone,
For thee I pine, for thee my heart doth groan,
If I've conceal'd my love, 'twas for thy sake,
So that no slur, thy enemies may make,
They may intrigue, their plots will go awry
For thee alone I live, for thee I'll die.
Oh! tell me love, yea, tell me of thy grace,
Where near thee I can be? Where is the place?
I would be by thy side to ever stay,
Even an inch is far too far away;
My heart is thine, with thee it ever goes,
Though rack'd with pain, for fear of jealous foes.
Many and strong are enemies of thine;
That direful distance we are kept apart,
Doth whirl my brain, with sorrow fill my heart.
Oh for a friend! one who could say to you,
He is thy slave, he ever loves thee true,
For want of thee, 'tis sure that I could die,
Take not the fault on thee, nor damp thy eye,
Thou art too frail, to such a burden share,
I take it all, I will the burden bear;

And on the Judgment Day, I'll loud proclaim,
My love is pure, on me be all the shame!
What pretexts I did make to gain a chance,
For e'en a moment, on thy form to glance;
But now, what, can I do? No pretext left,
Not an excuse! Of all I am bereft;
For to thy country, thou alas! art gone,
And I am left disconsolate, alone;
None have I left, a note to thee to take,
What can I do? My heart will surely break!
Oh happy thought! Myself, I will disguise,
And follow thee, and when the chance arise,
I'll snatch thee for my own, together fly.
And in some distant land, then, you and I
Will find a nest, where, like two turtle doves,
We'll live rejoicing in our mutual loves.[1]

1   Léon, "Ibn At-Tathriyya", *IC*, 1930, Vol.4, No.4, pp.581–2; possibly Léon's poetic rendition of
    Slane, Vol.IV, p.263. Attributed al-Tathriyya, as quoted by the poet Abu Tamman at-Ta'i.

UNTITLED (1930D)

Oh what would I do, what sacrifice make!
For one whom I love, for her own sweet sake,
Whose cool hand, if pass'd light o'er my head,
Would all my pain heal, bring life to the dead.
My life to devote to one, who me fears,
Whose doubt and whose love is mingled with tears,
I fear her also and fearfully dread,
That I am not lov'd, but another instead;
No favour she grants me; Oh hopeless task!
But from her I ne'er a favour will ask;
And, yet, I still hope and fervently pray,
That, united in love, we shall ever stay.[1]

1   Léon, "Ibn At-Tathriyya", *IC*, 1930, Vol.4, No.4, p.584, possibly Léon's poetic rendition of
     Slane, Vol.IV, p.263. In the *Kitab al-Aghani*, Abu'l-Faraj al-Isfahani formed a *Diwan* of Ibn al-
     Tathriyya's poetry, and attributes this to him.

UNTITLED (1930E)

Before Allah would I blush, my cheeks would be red,
If to my discredit, with truth, it were said,
To some other fond lover I did succeed,
And I was the second on her love to feed,
Or that while professing fond love, that she
Should be, with other, sharing favour with me
Or that my belov'd any favour should give
To any other, all the days I should live.
Am I then so base, that of me you could think
From the lake of love with another I'd drink?
My path must be private, secluded and sweet
Not an open *tank* trod by other feet.
I am not a suitor for love that's impure,
Or for affection that's too weak to endure,
I do long for love, for it I fondly call
I want it for ever, and I want it all.
Pure water is good and is sweet to the taste,[1]
And is drunk with pleasure, e'en when in haste;
But when mix'd with dregs, or beclouded with mud,
'Tis nauseous indeed, and to drink it who would?
A vile faithless woman from me I e'er thrust,
Zâniyat, fâhishat,[2] fills me with disgust.[3]

---

1   Léon notes that this final section is added in a version of the poem related by another author.
2   *Zâniyat*, fornicatress; *fâhishat*, a prostitute.
3   Léon, "Ibn At-Tathriyya", *IC*, 1930, Vol.4, No.4, p.585; possibly Léon's poetic interpretation
    of Slane, Vol.IV, pp.263–4. It is related by the traditionist Abu'l Hasan al-Mu'ayyad ibn
    Muhammad ibn 'Ali al-Tusi that these were Ibn al-Tathriyya's verses.

UNTITLED (1930F)

Many strive for a thing, but it cannot obtain,
Yet it cometh to others without care or pain;
How for favours, so small, men persistently toil,
To see, with dismay, someone else take the spoil;
Or when hope is all crush'd, and the favour they gain,
Find it to be useless and their labour all vain.[1]

1   Léon, "Ibn At-Tathriyya", *IC*, 1930, Vol.4, No.4, p.585; possibly Léon's poetic interpretation of
     Slane, Vol.IV, p.264. The traditionist al-Tusi also confirms these verses as Ibn al-Tathriyya's.

UNTITLED (1930G)

There is a stone which to it iron draws,
(Its innate magic virtue is the cause);
There is a maiden whose sweetness and light,
Is magic stronger than loadstone's might.
I try, against my will, from her to turn
This very act makes my love stronger burn.
When she is absent, then I close my ear,
Lest her name mention'd I should hap to hear,
For if I heard her name, such is the fact,
That name, like loadstone, swift would me attract,
And casting prudence, care, whate'er betide,
At once, in frenzy, hasten to her side.
Until I saw her, virgin was my heart,
I knew not love, with me it had no part,
But when I saw her, like *silsilat*[1] dart,
Hot love did strike to my most inmost heart.[2]

---

1   *Silsilat*, chain, link.
2   Léon, "Ibn At-Tathriyya", *IC*, 1930, Vol.4, No.4, p.586; an extended poetic elaboration by Léon
    of what is found in Slane, Vol.IV, p.264. The traditionist al-Tusi confirms these verses as Ibn
    al-Tathriyya's.

TO HABIBAH

Oh what a thing is love? What mighty pain?
What will men not do a woman's love to gain?
And yet their strivings often are in vain.
Oh woman, woman! Thou art e'er man's bane!
Our thoughts, our passions, ever to thee tend,
And to obtain thee all our efforts bend;
So 'tis with me, Habîbah, for I long,
I sigh for thee, for thee I tune my song,
In all the world I see no form but thine,
My one desire is but to make thee mine;
Thy lovely face, as perfect it doth seem,
Anointed daily with the richest cream;
Thy ruby lips, when words they utter,
Are sweet as honey mix'd with butter,
Thy lovely milk-white teeth, in crescent bow,
Like string of shining pearls set in a row,
A glance from thee, a look from sparkling eyes,
Is like a gleam of fire, straight from the skies;
Oh! how I long to clasp thee to my heart,
Oh, wretched fate! that keeps us thus apart.[1]

---

1   Haroun Mustapha Léon, "Ibn At-Tathriyya—The Poet of the Dairy, Part II", *IC*, 1931, Vol.5,
     No.1, pp.52–70 (p.53); ascribed to Ibn al-Tathriyya.

UNTITLED (1931A)

Oh! mighty one, by Allah chosen, Islam's sceptre to sway,
To maiden's plea of innocence, give heed, I pray, this day.
I am not male, 'twas Allah's will that I a maid should be,
His will, also, that I should love in faith and purity.
Rich robes are thine, on throne thou sittest, but still a man thou art,
I wear attire, to baulk desire, and thus I play my part
In innocence of coarser things, to thus more knowledge gain,
Dost thou not learn new facts each day, thus o'er Islam to reign?
When love's well-timed, 'tis not a fault to give the heart full sway,
Else why did God, the merciful, implant in heart its ray?
My love is pure, 'tis not for man, but for the poet's lay
Sex love doth die, but love for art can never pass away;
Is it a crime, when Allah wills, this call thus to obey,
Caliph proclaim me innocent, oh! do not say me nay![1]

---

1   Léon, "Ibn At-Tathriyya Part II", *IC*, 1931, Vol.5, No.1, pp.54–5; a translated poem about
     Zaynab posing as the student Yusuf to get close to her love, Ibn al-Tathriyya, whose sister accuses
     him of being a girl and so Zaynab is taken in front of the caliph Al-Walid and pleads her case.

LA YUTASALLA (DISCONSOLATE)

The sun had set, the night had come, and darkness then did reign,
When from the *akhur*[1] then I heard, a moan as one in pain,
I hastened there, and lo, I saw a camel lying there,
He moan'd and cried, he groan'd and sighed, his heart was full of care,
"My faithful beast, what 'sturbs you thus, why have you moan'd and cried?"
"My *naqah*[2] gone, they've ta'en her hence."
      'Twas thus what he replied.
"She is my mate, for her I wait, she is my loving wife.
To take her hence gives me offence, and cuts me like a knife,
I cannot eat, I cannot sleep, without my *naqah* dear,"
Again he moan'd, again he groan'd and from his eye the tear
Gush'd forth again, as when the rain doth pour from thunder-cloud,
And then his voice gave utterance, to cry so fierce and loud.
"Oh *naqah* come, I want thee so, Give heed unto my cry,
To thee I vow, I'm lonesome now, without thee I shall die!"
His moans and groans, his mouth that foams, did pierce me to the heart,
What shame it is, I thought sadly, two loving hearts to part,
And to the camel then I spoke and thus tried to console,
For truth to tell, I knew full well, a thorn was in his soul.
"Have patience do, alone not you, my poor brute, in your grief,
For men do grieve, and women too, and cannot find relief,
'Tis very sad, alas! 'tis bad; but 'tis decree of Fate,
That of the two, loving and true, the day comes soon or late,
When one must go, and leave in woe, a loving one behind,
It may be Death, it may be Fate, that snaps the cords that bind.
But we can hope to meet once more, and in that hope we trust."
He turn'd his head, and then he said, "Thanks for your words so true.
Your Prophet great, he once did state, that *we* are people too,
And if for men, I think that then, *haywanat*[3] may aspire,
In future state, with their own mate, to have what they desire."
The faithful steed may hope indeed in Garden sweet to dwell.
Allah is just, and therefore must reward all us as well.[4]

---

1   *Akhur*, a stable.
2   *Naqat*, a female camel.
3   *Haywanat*, animals.
4   Léon, "Ibn At-Tathriyya Part II", *IC*, 1931, Vol.5, No.1, pp.59–60; much elaborated compared
     to Slane, Vol.IV, p.265, and redolent of Quilliam's predilection for nonsense verse. Al-Marzubani
     relates through Abu'l-Jaysh that Ibn al-Tathriyya composed these lines.

FUNERAL SONG FOR IBN AL-TATHRIYYA

'Tis of the dead, beloved dead, that now I sing,
Of voice now silent, that, in verse, was once the King;
No single maid enshrin'd herself within his heart,
He lov'd, not one, but all, the whole and not the part;
His brain ne'er clouded he with fiery mad'ning wine,
His verse flow'd as a stream, sprung from a source divine,
For money, ne'er cared he, he scorned all such dross,
He never stooped to gain it and never mourned its loss
No enemy made he, to all he was a friend,
No slander e'er spoke he, the slandered he'd defend.
Two buds upon one stalk, twin children of one mother,
Together we were born, a sister and her brother,
Together, reverence to our parents, we e'er gave,
By love united we from cradle to his grave!

Art thou, my brother, then, for ever fled?
Must I then mourn, in unavailing woe,
For thee, my brother, number'd with the dead?
Thy lips, with eloquence, no longer flow,
Thy soothing voice, my heart no longer cheers,
All now, for me, is left, anguish and tears.[1]

---

1   Léon, "Ibn At-Tathriyya Part II", *IC*, 1931, Vol.5, No.1, p.70: Ascribed to Zaynab bint al-
Tathriyya, a *marthiya* (a mourning or funeral song) for her brother, Ibn al-Tathriyya.

UNTITLED (1931B)

When the breeze begins to blow,
I charge it with an ardent message
From a passionate lover to the presence of his beloved.
For my life I would sacrifice to her,
For she it is whose aspect gives life to our souls,
And whose presence perfumes and gives joy to the world.
I swear that since the time she departed,
I left untouched my wine-cup;
It was absent from me, because she was absent.
My passion for her never dies,
Approaching in the dark hour of midnight,
Unseen by watchful, jealous spies.[1]

---

1   Henri Mustapha Léon, "A Great Muslim Astrologer", *IC*, 1931, Vol.5, No.3, pp.434–41 (p.440).
      By 'Ali ibn Yunus, a great Egyptian astrologer and a prolific poet; a literal translation by Léon.

UNTITLED (1931C)

I wrote to 'Utbah and said Oh Love! think,
And assuredly know that on the brink
Of Jehennam I stand, trembling and lone,
And all on account of your heart of stone;
My eyes swim in tears, like fountain they gush,
In them, I'm immers'd, so fiercely they rush;
So great my affection, that I am in pain,
Unless you consent, my woes will remain,
This pain is for you, my love, my desire,
No waters, how deep, can quench my soul's fire!
Tired, at last, of my piteous wail,
That of a supplicant doomed to fail,
Doleful as wretch of each coin bereft,
And mournful as one, whom all hope had left,
Her cold heart was touch'd, she anxiously said,
"Does anyone know, or dumb as the dead,
Have you secret kept, of what you have told
In verses to me of your love so bold?"
Now what could I say? I must own the truth,
Yet I felt shamefac'd, just like one uncouth,
To own thus, that I instead of conceal,
In madness, to all, my love did reveal,
To love is no crime, whatever betide,
The raptures of love, sure, no one can hide,
But I had done more, alas! to my shame,
I had revealed my beloved's name!
"You wretch", she exclaim'd, then saying no more,
The casement she clos'd and banged the door.
And thus I am left, disconsolate, lone.
Oh, 'Utbah, belov'd! your heart is of stone.[1]

---

1   Haroun Mustapha Léon, "Abu'l-Atahiya, 'Al-Jarrar': The Poet Who Sold Earthen-Pots", *IC*,
1931, Vol.5, No.4, pp.631–50 (p.632); cf. greatly elaborated by comparison with Slane, Vol.I,
p.203. The celebrated poet, Isma'il ibn al-Qasim (748–825/6CE), whose poetic moniker was
Abu'l-'Atahiya (Father of Craziness), and who bore the nickname, "Al-Jarrar", the pot-seller or
jar-seller. He was famous for the violent passion he bore for a slave-girl, 'Utba, of the Caliph
Muhammad al-Mahdi's cousin, Rayta, for whom the great bulk of his love poems were written,
see "Abu'l-'Atāhiya", *EI2*, http://dx.doi.org/10.1163/1573-3912_islam_SIM_0161, accessed 1
July 2021.

UNTITLED (1931D)

There is one thing on earth I madly desire,
That quickens my pulse, sets my soul all afire,
The fulfilment of whereof on Allah depends,
And upon Al-Mahdi, with all it portends;
Yet my heart is gloomy and full of despair,
And so to you, Kaliph, I thus make my pray'r,
On earth, the maintainer of Allah's commands,
The Emir of Islam and far distant lands,
The world and its riches, thou reckon but dross,
Thy word is the law, no one would dare to cross,
Renown'd for thy Justice, thy subjects all thrive
In appealing to thee, my hopes then revive
Oh to me give 'Utbah! to take for her wife,
And thus quench my desire and give me new life![1]

---

1   Léon, "Abu'l-Atahiya", *IC*, 1931, Vol.5, No.4, pp.632–3; cf. greatly elaborated by comparison
     with Slane, Vol.I, p.203. Abu'l-Atahiya then writes to the caliph of his desire to obtain 'Utba
     from him.

UNTITLED (1931E)

O 'Omar! Mighty man, whose deeds inspire
The poet's soul and all his feelings fire,
An evil eye, sure now, o'er me has pass'd,
And all my hopes to disappointment cast
And evil influence on thee has shed,
That generosity has died or fled.
Where is the charm, or where can there be found,
In *hamayil*,[1] in air, in fire, or ground,
Whose pow'r so strong the evil can dispel,
Avert that eye and its effect expel?
Verse after verse will I pen line by line,
In language sweet, with thoughts that seem divine,
Until the shaytân, with its evil eye,
Grows tir'd and weary, and from thee doth fly;
If all this fail and ill thou still remain,
There, yet, is one, that's never us'd in vain,
Falaq wa Nas[2] ten thousand times I'll say,
'Omar, restor'd, will once more be himself,
And order that the poet have his pelf.[3]

---

1   *Hamayil*, amulet.
2   *Falaq wa Nas*, the last two chapters of the Qur'an.
3   Léon, "Abu'l-Atahiya", *IC*, 1931, Vol.5, No.4, p.636; cf. greatly elaborated by comparison with Slane, Vol.I, p.204. Abu'l-'Atahiya wrote to a patron, the governor (wali) 'Umar ibn al-A'la, complaining of his tardiness in rewarding him for a previous eulogy.

UNTITLED (1931F)

What is the matter? *Ma huwa'l ma'na?*
What is the reason she keeps me so far?
My mistress is cold, I woo her in vain,
She is so haughty, holds me in disdain.
The Khalifah advanced to him, with pomp and pride,
For this post he was the one, there was none beside
Alone for him was it fit, he alone for it.
His will the law to which all cheerfully submit;
If any other one for such post did aspire,
The sea, with horror, would go dry, and vomit fire;
The earth would tremble and the solid mountains shake,
The sun grow pale and dim and all the planets quake;
If e'en our inmost thoughts, from him, a moment stray
'Twould be a sin, thus fragrantly, to disobey.
For such a fearful sin, heavy and hard as stone,
What would Allah require as good deeds to atone?[1]

---

1   Léon, "Abu'l-Atahiya", *IC*, 1931, Vol.5, No.4, p.637; cf. greatly elaborated by comparison with
Slane, Vol.I, pp.204–5. Abu'l-'Atahiya recited these verses to the caliph Al-Mahdi.

UNTITLED (1931G)

Ikhwân![1] I am dying, 'Tis love that is causing my death!
Announce to the tomb, the approach of one yielding his breath,
Get ready the *kafan*,[2] Oh! grant to me, quickly, this boon,
For on the *tabut* my *jifat*[3] will be stretched very soon.
Reproach me not for dying, blame me not for submitting,
For the love that consumes me, there's nothing more fitting;
Sallam halaho![4] Myself I yield up, let death be my bride,
My life is a blank! less, otherwise, 'Utbah doth decide.[5]

---

1 Ikhwân, brothers; corrected from Akhwân.
2 *Kafan*, shroud.
3 *Tabut*, bier; *jifat*, corpse.
4 *Sallam halaho!*, Yield up oneself.
5 Léon, "Abu'l-Atahiya", *IC*, 1931, Vol.5, No.4, p.639; cf. greatly elaborated by comparison with Slane, Vol.I, p.206. These are verses Abu'l-'Atahiya wrote on his love for 'Utba. Léon gives a few other similar examples of the Abbasid poet's love poetry that have been omitted here to avoid repetition.

AL-KABILIYAT (THE TALENTS)

To me, Allah, *al Karim*,[1] did certain talents give,
To exercise those talents, sure, 'twas thus I came to live;
To let those talents rest unus'd and perish in the dust,
Sure 'tis a sin 'gainst Allah to betray such sacred trust,
Away such false impression, as dark before the light,
I'll live as Allah willeth, and verses still I'll write.[2]

---

1 *Al Karim*, the Generous, the Munificent, one of the ninety-nine names and attributes of Allah.
2 Léon, "Abu'l-Atahiya", *IC*, 1931, Vol.5, No.4, pp.649–50; lines that Abu'l-'Aahiya wrote in
   response to a fanatical mullah who had ordered him to give up poetry.

UNTITLED (1931H)

When my existence has expired and flown,
'Tis few who will sigh and still less who will groan,
The women who weep and exhibit their grief,
Will make lamentations, all short, curt and brief;
My comrade and friend, will of me cease to think,
My love, he'll forget, and his mem'ry will shrink,
He'll look for another, and when one he find,
My name and my love will quick fade from his mind.[1]

---

1   Léon, "Abu'l-Atahiya", *IC*, 1931, Vol.5, No.4, p.650; Abu'l-'Atahiya's own poem sung to him
on his deathbed by the famed Abbasid court musician Mukhariq.

BV - #0057 - 021221 - C0 - 234/156/15 - PB - 9781912356898 - Gloss Lamination